the crane bag

ogham oils and essences

by róisín carroll

Published by Irish Ogham Publications

(First published in Ireland in 1991
by Feasibility Publications)

© 1997 Róisín Carroll

Róisín Carroll
Irish Ogham Publications
The Ogham Apothecary
Carlingford, Co. Louth
Ireland

Telephone: +353 (0)42-73793

Fax: +353 (0)42-73839

ISBN 0-9531863-0-X

TABLE OF CONTENTS

To Feet

This book might not have been possible without the wonderful experiences I and my clients have had with Reflexology. I have found that Reflexology opens the passageways of the body to one's own healing. Through this self-healing, further doorways are opened to inner wisdom and self-knowledge. I feel I need to acknowledge my gratitude and thanks for the gifts I have received through Reflexology. To the people I have treated and to the people I have taught and who have taught me, I would like to say, "The best is yet to be."

ACKNOWLEDGMENTS

My deepest thanks to:

- Happi Mikki McQuirk, my talented editor, who wrote the descriptions, argued with the computer and did the design and layout. Her untiring, creative input was invaluable.

- The Tree Council of Ireland for the use of the artwork of the trees and for their guidance.

- Findhorn Foundation who are doing such inspirational work with nature.

- My clients and students who helped me grow.

- Therapists and colleagues for their nurturing and encouragement, especially Martina, Valerie, Tom, Mary and Joan.

- My staff at the Celtic Tree Oils, Ltd. who carried on while I worked on this vastly expanded edition.

- Trees for the way in which they have shown me unity and wholeness.

- My guides and teachers who wisely taught me so much along the Path.

- My mother (Mary Mulholland) for her strength and dedication.

- My father (Felix Mulholland) who inspired a love of nature in me.

- My sons (Dónal, Gearóid and Shane) and daughters (Caitriona, Sinéad and Caoimhe) for teaching me so much about myself.

- And, most of all, my husband, Gerry, for his loving support, his love of nature and his dedication to planting and growing.

IF

If I could be a tree,
I'd shade the world with tender care
And, in the dawn of Summer's day,
I'd house the birds their eggs to lay.

If I could be a crystal bright,
Shining in the dark of night,
I'd see hopes brighten, loads lighten,
In the search for soul's insight.

If I could be a flower gay,
I'd feed a bee in the month of May
And watch with joy as souls enjoy
My perfume sweet and colour bright.

If I could be a rainbow new,
Shining into eyes not yet blue,
I'd see new form unfold
With limitation untold.

If I could be a teardrop warm,
Healing wounds deeply borne,
I'd fill my heart with love untorn
And ponder the wonder of it all.

If I could be a breath of Spring,
I'd breathe new life into everything,
Watch the growth of pastures new
And catch a glimpse of God in dew.

If only I had eyes to see,
I am the shady tree, the crystal bright,
The flower gay, the rainbow new,
I am the teardrop warm, the breath of Spring, the
love of God.

The garden must be prepared
in the soul first
or else it will not flourish.

INTRODUCTION

In 1983, I was very ill and had several operations which were not successful. They depleted my energy. I was so sick that I wasn't fit to get up to do my normal work (at that time) of caring for and looking after the family. I had been on several doses of antibiotics which had made me feel very tired and dejected. I did at one stage think that I was actually going to die as I had lost all interest in life and was continually depressed.

However, one morning while in a semi-conscious state, I inwardly knew that the basis of my problem was that I wasn't taking responsibility for myself and for my own life. That particular day, I read an article in the Irish Times on complementary medicine. I decided I would start with homeopathy to treat myself in order to get well. I found an excellent homeopathic practitioner who helped me. I used homeopathic remedies and other complementary therapies.

After a couple of years, my life had changed because my health had changed. I began to feel more alive. I regained my interest in life. Then, I decided that I would change many things, including the way we ate. I decided at that time that I would train myself in some of these therapies. I chose Reflexology (treatment through massage of the feet) as my first love.

Having trained, I worked with family and friends in the beginning. Soon there was a path worn to my door. I eventually decided to set up professionally. The results were fascinating for me. I began to see how people were benefiting from what I was doing and then decided, since I was the only one in the area at the time, that what the community needed was more people to do what I was doing.

With this in mind, I set up a school which I had accredited both in Ireland and England by the professional bodies: The Irish Institute of Reflexology and the Association of Reflexology in England. By this time, I was also teaching in Belfast, Northern Ireland.

This work gave me wonderful insight into the problems of divided communities and helped me to develop myself as well seeing how these communities could be helped. I also realized that every student I taught could bring these skills back to alleviate stress in their communities. In this way, I saw that my work was very necessary to aid in creating peace and healing within individuals and the wider population.

I had, through the years, also been using the Bach Flower Remedies which gave me insight into trees, plants and herbs. Further understanding came to me as to how the trees could help the

physical body. By now, the ground was set for my initial "meeting" with the trees of the Ogham system.

THE TREES TALK TO ME

I was playing golf one day with my husband. My golf ball went into the Hawthorn hedge. I went in to look for the ball. While I was in there, I actually sensed what the Hawthorn could do in the body. At that time, I was suffering with disturbances in my lymphatic system. I could feel the Hawthorn affecting my lymph glands through a tingling sensation in my body. Needless to say, I was surprised and amazed. Yet, I also felt that I had made a friend for life and I wanted to share this discovery with others.

Over the next few years, I had personal experiences with many different trees which I wrote down. With all of them, I sensed in my own body how they could help on different levels, including the physical. As the years went by, I began wondering what I would do with this information.

Then, in a dream one night, I saw the Ogham* symbols with the trees. At that time, there were

• •

* Ogham is pronounced Aum – the Universal Cosmic Note. In Irish, Ogham is spelled Oǧam. The buailte (dot above the consonant) was dropped from the written language with the introduction of typewriters. The Irish version carries a higher vibration.

some symbols that I didn't recognize as being part of what I knew to be the ancient, traditional Ogham alphabet as written on the stones (Ogham Stones are generally found on sacred sites in Ireland and other Celtic countries). Nonetheless, I recorded this dream information. As a result of the dream, I started asking within what I was to do with these symbols.

Later, in another dream, I saw trays full of bottles. As I woke from my dream, the word "oil" was sounding in my ears. I then realized that some process needed to be gone through with the trees in order to convert their energies and qualities into a form that could be used for healing in all areas. At that point, I didn't know what that process was.

During all this period, I took various courses in colour therapy and trained with the now world-famous and well-respected Vicky Wall of Aura Soma. I remember her saying to me one day to go into the hedgerows. She didn't say why. Later on, this statement made sense to me when one day I was standing looking at rose hips and suddenly remembered what she said. The rose hip, when I held it, told me that it would be very good to use for the reproductive area of the body. That experience was the catalyst and beginning of a whole new phase of my work.

I had a clear insight that each tree in some way represented archetypal qualities of people and the various systems in their bodies. Eventually, through a number of intuitive processes, I came to settle on the distillation of the trees and plants that make up the Ogham Tree Oils and Essences* which use mostly the bark of the trees. The plant material is gathered at certain times of the year when the energy is highest and in conjunction with beneficial planetary timing.

People often ask me if these Oils and Essences are the same as the Bach Flower Remedies. My answer is: this work I have done is pioneering work. It is a progression of Dr. Bach's work. However, Dr. Bach never mentioned the physical body. My work, on the other hand, does address the health of the physical body as well as the emotional, mental, spiritual and etheric bodies. As in many other areas of science, art and medicine, we stand on the shoulders of giants as we progress in awareness and knowledge for our own time.

Further intuitive flashes led to the development of cards with the corresponding characteristics of the trees, Ogham symbols and meanings which will be revealed later in this book.

● ●

* These Oils and Essences may support healing of disturbances of energy of the systems of the body. If symptoms persist, consult a medical practitioner.

Since I honour the Earth, all creation and appreciate the plants that have given their lives for this healing work, I make sure that three times as much as I use in processing the oils and essences is replanted. My husband, who is attuned to the plant kingdom, has taken on the responsibility for this planting and in so doing helps to give birth to the new forest.

The discovery process continues. For example, the trees have recently revealed to me that they were once walking people. Like many other neighbours, they sometimes have their differences and preferences. Still being revealed to me are the notes for each tree, the song/symphony of the trees, how they play and interact with the wind and the other elements, how they can forecast the weather and what their connections are with each other.

And now, I'd like to invite you to journey with me through the trees and see what they say to you. There is no right or wrong in this discovery process. Your experience of the trees will be your very own. Please consider the information in this book as a guide. We are all learning from each other. I have shared some of my experiences with you. In turn, I would enjoy hearing what your experiences are as you get to know and make friends with our leafy "companions."

TWO SWANS

Why did we fight?
What happened to our tree?
Where are the smiles
Of the courageous and free?

Deep in my soul,
I know we are old,
Floundering, trying,
To come in from the cold.

In the dark of the night
Will there ever be light?
I look to the sea
For comfort and sight.

Two swans have
Come to visit me.
"A sign!" I say of the new day.
"Courage my child. Hold firm in the disarray."

A whole day you stay
And I watch you play,
Court each other in permanency.
My faith is renewed.

In love and hope,
I stand and wait at the Temple Door
For the trumpet
To sound and Angels' song,

Bidding us enter
the Majestic Hall,
Where peace reigns
Since before the Fall.

Thank you, two swans.
Now you fly away,
Leaving me stronger
And able to face the New Day.

THE CRANE BAG

St. Columcille was known as the Crane Cleric due to his wisdom. When he was living on Iona Island, a crane landed one day with a broken wing. Columcille asked some people to look after the crane and to come to him when the crane's wing was better. They did so. Columcille then said to let the crane go free and let it fly back to Derry from whence it had come to visit him in exile.

This story inspired the name of The Crane Bag. When I was first starting to work with the Ogham alphabet symbols, I had a local artist carve a set of symbols onto pieces of wood so that I could study them and learn how to work with them. To keep them with me at all times, I had a bag knitted from Aran wool to carry them around in. While contemplating their wisdom one day, I was visited by a crane which reminded me of the Columcille story. Cranes, as they fly, make symbols with their feet. The idea then came to me to call this system "The Crane Bag."

The "Crane Bag" is the complete Ogham (see below). The Ogham is the story of the Tree in the spiritual, emotional, mental and physical being of us. It reaches into the depths of understanding, so profound, and yet so simple. The Ogham embodies the wisdom of the ages and the sages.

The Ogham of itself just IS. The Ogham poses many questions and allows us the space in which to ponder. As we think about the Ogham, every answer begs another question.

To feel and be in tune with all the elements of the Tree is to be alive. Eavesdropping on the conversation of trees is to grow in awareness. To hear the messages the wind carries with it as it blows through the Tree is food for the soul.

THE CELTIC PEOPLE

The Celtic peoples are supposed to have originated in Northwest India through Asia Minor thousands of years ago. Their migrations took them through many countries over the centuries. Traces of Celtic symbolism have been found in Africa, throughout Europe and other continents. Eventually, the Celts made their way to Ireland bringing with them a sophisticated system of law, bardic lore and understanding of symbolism (artistic creations).

According to ancient Druid and early Irish Christian laws (known as the *Bretha Comaithchesa* meaning Laws of the Neighborhood – also as Brehon Laws), trees, shrubs and bushes were protected. A penalty was incurred for the unlawful felling of a tree and the penalty matched the severity of the crime. Under the laws, trees had

four different hierarchical statuses: *airig fedo* (nobles of the wood), *aithig fedo* (commoners of the wood), *fodla fedo* (lower divisions of the wood) and *losa fedo* (bushes of the wood). For example, if an Oak (noble of the wood) was illegally cut down, a penalty of two and a half milk cows had to be paid. If a neighbor's furze (bush of the wood) was cut, the penalty was a yearling heifer.

As we look at the way the Celts lived and how they related to each other and their environment, we become aware of the wealth of knowledge and wisdom left behind. For those who are prepared to search, this knowledge and wisdom is waiting but the search must start in the "Earth" of ourselves.

In the search for the Inner Self, we may feel the need for the use of images and symbolism. Celtic Mythology has a wealth of symbolism which has stirred the imagination of people down through the ages.

OGHAM

To understand the significance of the Ogham (alphabet of the Celtic people), we need to look at what it was and is. There is first of all a hint that this system of knowledge was used not only by the Celts but also by many other peoples of

the Ancient World. Somehow in Ireland, the Ogham knowledge has survived in the psyche of the Irish people and at this time is being re-discovered.

Ogham was an ancient way of communicating – an alphabet. It is a language of symbols which holds a deep meaning. Each letter carries a host of ideas relating to the Celtic philosophy of the trees. There are forty of these symbols which are the complete Ogham. Thirteen of these were used as the Celtic Tree alphabet calendar. The Celtic year consisted of thirteen months, thirteen moons and a tree related to each month. Beith (Birch) is the first month of the Celtic year, for instance.

The Celtic Great Lunar Year was a cycle of nineteen years. This Great Year started with a New Moon at the beginning of the Celtic year. Since each cycle of the Moon does not quite equal a month, it takes the full cycle of nineteen years to bring another New Moon at the Celtic New Year. This fact makes it difficult to correlate the Moon phase with our current Solar calendar. Therefore, in this book, the months associated with the thirteen sacred trees should be considered approximate.

Since the Celts lived close to the natural world, they found a balance in this harmony with their

environment, respecting all creation. Since we have lost this balance with ourselves and with our environment, we need to find ways of bringing harmony back into our lives, through embracing and caring for the whole. Within the Ogham, we find the symbolism that can bring us further along in awareness on our spiritual path in a way that's personal and revealing.

NAMES

Many places and people in Ireland are named after trees. Derry (Doire), for example, was named after the Oak (Duir) because Derry was once an oak forest. Another example is found in Kilsallagh meaning Willow (Saille) Wood. The surname Coll derives from the Celtic name for Hazel.

HISTORY & WEATHER

Trees can teach us our history. They record what is actually happening on the planet in terms of plague, disease, hard winters, floods, etc. In years where there has been some identifiable human disaster, the trees have recorded less growth. The trees suffer the same disaster and are affected through the destructive vibrations around them in the atmosphere.

Trees can also be a barometer of the weather to come. Here are some examples. When the un-

dersides of the leaves, particularly of Sycamore, Lilac and Poplar, turn up and give the impression of a light colour, it is a sure sign of rain. If the wind has a hollow sound among the trees, it is also a sign of rain. The cones of some evergreen trees open up when the weather is going to be good and close when bad weather is imminent. It is said of the Blackthorn that, if there comes a bitterly cold spell coinciding with its flowering, that it is a "Blackthorn Winter." The Oak and the Ash have a rhyme to help us: "If the Oak is out before the Ash, then you'll only get a splash. But, if the Ash is out before the Oak, then you can expect a soak."

LEY LINES AND THEIR EFFECTS ON TREES

Earth is a sentient being and has a pulse. Her nervous system (ley lines) grids the planet. At the places where these ley lines cross, vortices of energy are found. Sometimes, there is a disturbance of these energies – perhaps due to radiation (natural or man-made), fault lines, magnetic deposits or other irregularities in the crust. The energy underground affects the shapes of trees. For example, if a tree grows over a disturbed vortex or ley line, it may become twisted or dwarfed. Alternatively, if the energy is harmonious at such locations, the tree will be healthy, strong and possibly larger than normal. We are also affected by these energies – feeling good in

a congenial location and uncomfortable where the energy is upset.

In Ireland, pilgrimages in olden times followed the ancient Atlantean energy lines. Hawthorns were planted along these lines. I believe that an artifact of those times is the radon gas leftover from the destruction of Atlantis.*

BIRDS

A special, nurturing relationship exists between birds and trees and is a delight to watch. Because of their dependence on each other (in part, at least, for survival), they are a perfect example of symbiosis and inter-species cooperation. Birds shelter and build their homes in trees. Trees spread their seeds partly by feeding the birds. I have noticed how particular birds visit certain types of trees over and over again. For example, the Cross-bill feeds off of pine seeds. The shape of its beak has evolved specifically to pry open pinecones to get at the seeds.

Seeing a connection between the medicine of the trees and the medicine of the birds, I included

• •

*With today's more air-tight houses, radon gas has become a problem as it seeps up through the ground level into homes. Occurrences of cancer have risen in radon-rich areas which have a high incidence of non-circulating, enclosed environments. This gas is not dangerous in the open air.

birds and some of their lore as an expression of their connection. Birds have often appeared to me at meaningful times. Birds have their own messages. I offer these associations for you to contemplate.

PLANETS

Astrology is perhaps the most ancient of all sciences. Many astrologers through the centuries (Culpeper, for example) have associated the different planets with various elements, such as colours, crystals, numbers as well as trees and plants. A brief description follows of the different planets and their meanings along with the Celtic god or goddess that is associated with each.*

THE SUN   LUGH
The true spirit or Self of each of us, the source of will, vitality, personal power, personality, ego, qualities of leadership and authority, purpose and direction in life

MOON   BRIGID, DANU AND MACHA
The emotional body and the feeling nature, (gut) reactions, instincts, the body, the mother, bio-psychic functions, nourishment, protection, assistance, adaptation

••••••••••••••••••••••••••••••••••

* There are around 400 gods and goddesses in Ireland alone. These designations are my own correlations.

MERCURY   **ANGUS OG**

Education, communication, the mental field, thought processes, perception, the intellect, interchange, association, (use of) knowledge, reason

VENUS   **TRIPLE GODDESS (BANBA, FODHLA AND ERIU – THE LAND OF IRELAND) & BOANN (THE RIVER BOYNE – MOTHER OF ANGUS OG)**

The affections and the value nature, harmony, art, beauty, the ability to attract others and maintain relationship, communion, aesthetics, appreciation, inner meaning, internalisation

MARS   **THE MORRIGAN AND OGMA***

Energy, anger, war and warriors, force, will, aggressiveness, desire, passion, initiative, assertion, outwardly directed activity, externalisation

JUPITER   **DAGDA (THE GOOD)**

The expansive principle, opportunity, success, prosperity, compensation, assimilation, preservation, increase, self-sustaining, *dharma* (right action), wise counsellor, guru, patriarch, saviour, largeness, bigger than life, religion

••••••••••••••••••••••••••••••••••

* The eloquent, warrior god, Ogma, is credited with the invention of the Ogham.

SATURN   **NUADA OF THE SILVER HAND AND THE CAILLEACH**

Lessons to learn, structures, karma, authority, the great teacher, crystallisation, focalisation, differentiation, limitation, restriction, form, discipline, sorrow, hardships, the father, security

CHIRON   **DIANCECHT**

Health and healing, the physician, the bridge or gateway between the inner personal planets and the outer spiritual planets

URANUS   **MacCUILL, MacCECHT & MacGRENÉ**

Sudden and unexpected happenings, transformation, revolution, change, disruption, humanitarianism, the psychic realms, eccentricity, inventiveness, instability, creative genius, threshold knowledge and experiences

NEPTUNE   **LIR OR MANANNAN**

Universalisation, impressionability, spirituality, nebulousness, confusion, imagination, dissolution, inclusiveness, naiveté, escapism, illusion, irrationality, disappointment, deception, disillusionment, creativity

PLUTO   **BADHBH**

The underground, rejuvenation, (the spiritual) will, regeneration, transformation, power,

refocalisation, renewal, compulsion, elimination, power trips

COLOUR AND CRYSTALS

The healing power of crystals and colour is well known. Many books have been written on these subjects. Crystals and colour have been used through the ages and are mentioned several times in the Bible, especially in Revelations.

The Ogham Oils and Essences* carry the vibration of the crystals and colours. The gem and colour that are used are those best suited to bring out the subtlety of the oil or essence. By using the oils and essences, the energies of the colours and crystals are also being absorbed.

It is also possible to develop different qualities for yourself by wearing or carrying the appropriate crystal and surrounding yourself with a chosen colour. For example, red would provide energy, blue is calming and yellow is for joy and mental clarity.

• •

* These Oils and Essences may support healing of disturbances of energy of the systems of the body. If symptoms persist, consult a medical practitioner.

GREEN

Green upon my open door,
A welcome mat upon my floor,
Green in laughs and whispers gay
To soothe the troubles of the day.

Green in limes newly plucked,
And in apples sweetly sucked,
Kiwis surely are a treat
But what colour is bitter sweet?

From cities busy and concrete jungles,
Tired souls in numbers tumble,
To embrace the green of the gentle breeze
And the whisper of the green of trees.

A green note, sweetly sung in tune,
Soothes and bathes my vertebrae.
Green upon my lips to speak:
What colour was my speech today?

Green upon my eyelids light,
As I laugh away the night.
Green in other peoples eyes:
Which green do I see or are there sties?

Green in poker faces true,
Tomorrow green. Or are they blue?
Should I risk some other hues
To help me read incoming cues?

Earth turns green at dawn of Spring.

Green breathes new life into everything.
Green supports the flower bright
And keeps me balanced through the night.

How many greens upon the Earth?
Their smells, their tastes, their feel: a dream
To tired eyes, a welcome feast,
And, oh! to hear the sound of green.

St. Patrick's Shamrock came alive
As he told of timeless Trinity.
The grass of' Newgrange and Tara high
Lends new hope to Antiquity.

Green around my heart galore.
I need to keep an open door.
The green, prickly holly will help me be
Free of envy and jealousy.

Green in emerald healing me
In many ways I cannot see.
Green in emblems could mean more,
If I could understand my lore.

Transformation in the liver:
Will I fight, or will I quiver?
Green bile, will you help comfort me,
If I should let pride get hold of me?

Green in circles and crosses neat,
Bringing life to my feet
through flowing Waters in the deep
That fought for insight I may reap.

OGHAM OILS AND ESSENCES

The healing properties of oils are well known. The use of oils in healing is an ancient form of natural treatment documented as far back as five thousand (or more) years ago in such places as Egypt, China and Tibet. A favourite story is that of Mary Magdalen washing the feet of Jesus with her oils. Oils and Essences work on many subtle levels of the person and, like symbols, they work on the right brain or sub-conscious – the feminine aspect of ourselves. They are powerful, easy to use and a wonderful key to the unlocking of our inner resources.

Ogham Oils and Essences* have been carefully prepared from Irish trees under precise conditions. The harvesting of the wood and distillation of the Oils and Essences are a very special labour of love and a gift to humanity at this time.

The complete Crane Bag is comprised of Oils and Essences from forty trees, this book and a set of cards. On the cards, the medicine of each tree is represented by an Ogham symbol. Also included are: a keyword, the philosophy of each tree and the bodily system affected. These cards can be used as a teaching tool, a system of divination

These Oils and Essences may support healing of disturbances of energy of the systems of the body. If symptoms persist, consult a medical practitioner.

and as a way of tuning into the particular oil/ essence needed.

This book will provide full information about each tree, the systems of the body, how to use the oils and essences, divination techniques and the hand ogham. The hand ogham is a means of using the oils to access the link between the trees and each system of the body.

So, we welcome you to the world of Ogham Oils and Essences. It is a world full of surprises as you encounter yourself among the trees. The trees are the lungs of the Earth. Our lungs are the trees of the body. Our interaction with each tree and each Ogham Oil or Essence brings us a new surprise as we meet with different aspects of ourselves. Since trees have different person- alities, each tree we meet can mirror for us an aspect of ourselves.

We live in an age where we need to look at ill- ness in a wholistic way, taking all aspects of the person into consideration: physical, emotional, mental and spiritual. Since physical illness does not start in the physical body, we do need to look at the emotional, mental and spiritual states which we find ourselves in as we walk the path of life.

Since we carry the past, present and future of all these elements within us into every moment, there should be a constant change within us but, sometimes, change is difficult. In order that we may release blockages which may be causing illness or imbalance, it is recommended that three Ogham Oils or Essences* are used at a time, one to break past patterns, one to strengthen us in the Now and one to help us flow into the next phase of the Self.

So that the best results can be experienced from Ogham Oils and Essences, it is necessary to understand that ailments or disturbances (which are being experienced at any given time) are best treated according to the system of the body which is affected. For example, if the Respiratory System is the one affected, we recommend Ash, Ivy and Elder.

* These Oils and Essences may support healing of disturbances of energy of the systems of the body. If symptoms persist, consult a medical practitioner.

THE SYSTEMS OF THE BODY AND THE OGHAM OILS AND ESSENCES FOR EACH SYSTEM

There are ten systems in the body covering all of our physical organs and their energies. If we wish to cleanse and rejuvenate the whole system, we can do this by cleansing one system at a time. We recommend that you start with whatever system is most in need of being brought into balance. In order that we may understand how the Oils and Essences* effect change, it is best we understand in some detail how the body works. Like the fingers of the hand, there are ten systems which, while separate, all interact with each other.

CIRCULATORY SYSTEM

Circulation is a system of transportation. Through this system, the blood is pumped around the body carrying with it nutrients, hormones and oxygen. The extent to which we are in harmony with the Circulatory System of the Universe, or the Cosmic Flow, is the extent to which we our-

• •

* These Oils and Essences may support healing of disturbances of energy of the systems of the body. If symptoms persist, consult a medical practitioner.

selves will be free to experience the free flowing of our own blood. This system is one which connects all the others.

Serious disturbances of energy can be the result of toxic waste not being eliminated from the body so if the supply of blood to tissues and organs is restricted in any way damage may ensue. The heart itself has four chambers, two male and two female – which is perfect balance.

Some disturbances of energy in the Circulatory System: Angina, Palpitations, High and Low Blood Pressure, Thrombosis, Phlebitis, Varicose Veins Varicose Ulcers, Heartache (not allowing love to flow).

AFFIRMATION FOR THE CIRCULATORY SYSTEM: I allow love to flow freely through me.

CHARACTERISTICS: Nourishment, Centredness and Love.

LYMPHATIC SYSTEM

This system works very closely with the Circulatory System. Its function is to carry away the rubbish of the body which is too much for the blood stream. On the physical level, it literally carries away rubbish and on other levels it also does

the same. Blockages in the Lymphatic System could lead to a build up of toxins thus hindering the drainage of rubbish from cells, tissues and organs. The cleansing Hawthorn helps rid the body of a build up of rubbish in the Lymph Glands.

One of the differences between the Circulatory System and the Lymphatic System is that the blood is pumped by the heart but it is the breath that moves the lymphatic fluid. This fluid in turn bathes the cells, tissues and organs, cleansing and healing them. Here we see an example of the interconnection of systems, one depending on the other. What type of air did we breathe today?

Disturbances of energy in the Lymphatic System include Swollen Glands (which are located all over the body, as in the Tonsils, build up of Catarrh, Blood Poisoning, Flu, Oedema, Varicose Veins, Holding On To The Old, Neglect of the Intuition.

Affirmation for the Lymphatic System: I release that which no longer serves me.

Characteristics: Intuition, Empathy and Cleansing.

RESPIRATORY SYSTEM

Through Respiration our interaction with the trees is seen to be working most clearly. When we draw a breath, we breathe in life – the same life that is shared by everybody else on this planet. What we breathe out, the trees breathe in. Without the trees and plants, there would be no life on Earth because they produce oxygen. In the lungs, the exchange of gasses takes place making the lungs one of the points where macrocosm meets microcosm. The lungs are the trees of the body and the trees are the lungs of the Earth.

One of the functions of the Respiratory and Circulatory Systems is to supply the cells of the body with oxygen as we breathe in life and breathe out waste.

Some disturbances of energy of the Respiratory System are: Bronchitis, Pleurisy, Whooping Cough, Asthma, Emphysema, Chest Infection, Hay Fever, Laryngitis, Phlegm, Sore Throat, Ear Problems, Loss of Sense of Smell, Unable to Change with Life.

AFFIRMATION FOR THE RESPIRATORY SYSTEM: I breathe life easily and I speak my truth.

CHARACTERISTICS: Change, Freedom and Universal Truth.

THE SKIN

The skin is the mantle of the body and one of its functions is to protect the body. The skin is our outer connection with the macrocosm. Through the skin, we can feel the outer world. The skin sends messages constantly to the Nervous System so there is a wonderful liaison between the Nervous System and the skin. The skin secretes about one quarter of the waste products of the body. If there is a malfunction of the skin, the other organs of excretion will be under stress doing the job of the skin. If there is malfunction in the organs of excretion, the skin will be under stress. The skin absorbs oils but does not absorb water so treatment through the skin with oils will immediately affect the person on not only the physical level, but also emotionally, mentally, spiritually and etherically.

Some disturbances of the skin are: Psoriasis, Acne, Eczema, Boils, Warts, Sunburn, Ringworm, Shingles, Measles, Chickenpox, Shame, At Odds with the Environment, Not Feeling Protected.

AFFIRMATION FOR THE SKIN: I am protected in my environment.

CHARACTERISTICS: Change, Freedom and Universal Truth.

DIGESTIVE SYSTEM

The language we use unconsciously each day usually has a depth to it. "What is eating me up?" or "I couldn't stomach it" or "It stuck in my craw."

The Digestive System is about the digestion of food but, on other levels, it is also about digesting things. On an emotional level, not being able to digest something may lead to disturbances of energy in the Digestive System. The challenge is to let go emotionally. If we might have problems letting go of waste and unwanted material in the physical body, we may also have problems letting go on an emotional level.

Some disturbances of energy of the Digestive System: Flatulence, Colitis, Indigestion, Ulcers, Gall Stones, Jaundice, Diverticulitis, Cold Sores, Haemorrhoids, Appendicitis, Constipation, Diarrhea. Hernia, Malabsorbtion, Not Taking in Life's Lessons.

AFFIRMATION FOR THE DIGESTIVE SYSTEM: I let go of old patterns and absorb life's lessons with wisdom and joy.

CHARACTERISTICS: Confidence, Endurance and Tolerance.

MUSCULAR SYSTEM

The Muscular System speaks to us of elasticity, expansion and contraction. Each cell of the body carries the memory of what it is: the genetic memory and the blueprint of the whole. The Muscular System, like other systems, remembers the memories of the past. It remembers the friction, being too tight or too loose, being pulled this way and that way, physically, emotionally and spiritually. The muscle moves to give and take and ultimately find balance through this. The inner disharmony of conflicting thought processes may create the environment for a "pulled muscle." Tendons, ligaments and muscles work closely together. The tendons are the cords of the body, holding everything together. Disharmony in one may lead to disharmony in the other.

Some disturbances of the Muscular System: Muscular Atrophy, Frozen Shoulder, Rheumatism, Pulled Muscles, Immobility, Lack of Energy, Lumbago, Muscular Aches, Fibromyalgia, Sprains, Stiffness, Stuck in a Rut, Trapped Energy.

AFFIRMATION FOR THE MUSCULAR SYSTEM: I move forward with ease and grace.

CHARACTERISTICS: Expansion, Expression and Acceptance.

SKELETAL SYSTEM

The Skeleton is the physical frame of the body. The degree to which we are able to carry and deal with our burdens is the degree of well-being of the structure of the physical frame. Stiffness in joints may reflect stiffness of thought or a rigidity of mind. A weakness in the spine may reflect a lack of support now or in the past. Sacroiliac imbalance reflects an imbalance between the left and right sides of the body or between past and present, subconscious and conscious, masculine and feminine. Remembering the interconnectedness of all the systems, the processes of elimination have a big bearing on this system. Keeping the "house" clean delights the visitor.

Some disturbances of energy of the Skeletal System: Arthritis, Broken Bones, Scoliosis, Injury to the Frame, Back Problems, Fractures, Joint Problems, Slipped Disc, Compressed Vertebrae, Skeletal Problems, Stiffness in Mind and Body, Feeling Unsupported.

AFFIRMATION FOR THE SKELETAL SYSTEM: I am supported in life.

CHARACTERISTICS: Strength, Self-discovery and Surrender.

Nervous System

To embrace wholeness, we must look at physical, emotional, mental and spiritual well-being. Illness does not start in the physical body but on other levels since there is no separation between the different dimensions of ourselves. To balance and harmonise the Nervous System, we need space, nature, acknowledgment of our life's purpose, fulfillment and spiritual goals.

Some disturbances of the Nervous System: Depression, Insomnia, Migraine, Multiple Sclerosis, Shingles, Headaches, Emotional Disturbance, Meningitis, Anxiety, Epilepsy, Excessive Worry, Fear, Introversion, Mental Stress, Nervousness, Paranoia, Phobias, Feeling Out of Tune and Unable to Trust.

Affirmation for the Nervous System: I am at one with and trust the pulse of life.

Characteristics: Hope, Decisiveness and Simplicity.

GLANDULAR SYSTEM

The Glandular System is the link between the Divine World and the human world. The Master Gland, the Pituitary, leads the orchestra. If the leader of the orchestra is in harmony, the symphony is melodic. The beauty of the music may evade us if our Glandular System is out of tune. This system produces the hormones, the messengers of the body. When we are open to the Divine world, we can hear messages when they arrive and act accordingly.

The Glandular System and Nervous System work very closely together. The glands release the hormones directly into the bloodstream and they then travel to their appointed target.

Some disturbances of energy of the glandular System: Pre-menstrual Tension, Mood Swings, Fatigue of Adrenal Glands, Glandular Fever, Menopausal Problems, Mumps, Poor Metabolism, Postnatal Depression, Swollen Glands, Feeling Cut Off From the Spirit World.

AFFIRMATION FOR THE GLANDULAR SYSTEM: I am balanced between Spirit and Matter.

CHARACTERISTICS: Insight, Inspiration and Vision.

URINARY SYSTEM

Some of the functions of the kidneys, which form part of the Urinary System, are to regulate the body's water content, regulate the salt balance in the body, maintain the acid/alkali balance, filter the blood and help regulate blood pressure.

The Spirit of Life is the keyword of the kidneys. If we are fearful or stressed in life, we might develop imbalances in the kidney. Since many of the functions of the kidneys are about balance, we might need to look at these areas of our lives. Many hormones are produced by the Adrenal Glands which lie over the kidney. Some of these are Cortisone, Adrenaline and some male and female hormones. The bladder is the reservoir for urine or, put another way, for the waste water of the body. With problems of the bladder, it might be helpful to look at issues around control and unshed tears.

Some disturbances of energy of the Urinary System: Cystitis, Urethritis, Water Retention, Kidney Stones, Enuresis, Incontinence, Kidney Problems, Bladder Problems, Blame, Fear, Guilt, Not Going with the Flow.

AFFIRMATION FOR THE URINARY SYSTEM: I accept with courage the Divine Flow.

CHARACTERISTICS: Courage, Faith and Peace.

REPRODUCTIVE SYSTEM

Birth and death are part of the same cycle. The internal rhythm of the female cycle is a reflection of the outer lunar cycle with its differing phases. Moving through these phases with awareness brings us to an understanding of our own ebb and flow.

To give birth to a baby is one of the wonders of nature. Giving birth in the physical or human sense is one type of birth but there is also the wondrous renewal and rebirth of ourselves at different phases of our development. For health and harmony to prevail in this system, body, mind and spirit need to be integrated. If our relationship either with ourselves, others, or our environment is not nurturing and life-giving, disturbances of energy in the Reproductive System might be the result.

Some disturbances of energy in the Reproductive System: Pre-menstrual Tension, Amenorrhoea, Dysmenorrhoea, Menorrhagia, Endometriosis, Ovarian Cysts, Problems of the Prostrate Gland, Irregular Menstrual Cycle, Menopausal Problems, Menstrual Cramps, Sexual Problems, Thrush, Blockages of the Feminine/Masculine Aspects, Denying Creativity.

AFFIRMATION FOR THE REPRODUCTIVE SYSTEM: I am at one with my own creative source.

CHARACTERISTICS: Creativity, Resourcefulness and Renewal.

PANCREATIC

Because of the stress brought to bear on the Solar Plexus (and therefore, the Pancreas) as a result of such things as AIDS, Candida, Myalgic Encephalomyelitis (M.E.), Chronic Fatigue Syndrome, we have created a Pancreatic Oil and Essence. This Oil and Essence also treat: Blood Sugar Disturbances, Diabetes, Immune Deficiency Disorders, Disturbances of the Pancreas, including Pancreatitis, Feelings of Rejection, Loss of Sweetness in Life.

AFFIRMATION FOR THE PANCREAS GLAND: I accept the sweetness and abundance of life and I acknowledge my gifts.

CHARACTERISTICS: Insight, Courage, Decisiveness, Hope, Confidence, Protection and Centredness.

SINUSITIS

Disturbances in the environment have introduced many toxins into the air increasing problems with the sinuses. This situation has created a need for a special combination of oils and essences to treat sinusitis. This remedy also treats: Cold, Flu, Disturbances of the Sinuses, Loss of Sense of Smell, Allergies, Environmental Illnesses, Tinnitus, Vertigo, Headaches, Irritations, Disharmony in the Environment.

AFFIRMATION FOR THE SINUSES: I am at one with my environment.

CHARACTERISTICS: Intuition, Empathy, Cleansing, Change, Freedom, Universal Truth and Inspiration.

* These Oils and Essences may support healing of disturbances of energy of the systems of the body. If symptoms persist, consult a medical practitioner.

LIST OF SYSTEMS WITH
OGHAM OILS AND ESSENCES

Having looked at the systems, we can now look at the Ogham Oils and Essences* which benefit each system:

Circulatory System
1. Vine
2. Spindle
3. Honeysuckle

Lymphatic System
1. Hawthorn
2. Willow
3. Hazel

Respiratory System
   & Skin
1. Ash
2. Ivy
3. Elder

Digestive System
1. Beech
2. Oak
3. Sycamore

Muscular System
1. Birch
2. Alder
3. Sloe

Balancers
1. Reed
2. Grove
3. Magdalen
4. Weeping Willow
5. Rowan
6. Spiritual Rescue

Skeletal System
1. Blackthorn
2. Horse Chestnut
3. Holly

Nervous System
1. Heather
2. Apple
3. Furze

Glandular System
1. Silver Fir
2. Lilac
3. Sweet Pea

Urinary System
1. White Poplar
2. Pine
3. Copper Beech

Reproductive System
1. The Sea
2. Yew
3. Wild Rose

Auric –
   Subtle Bodies
1. Bog Myrtle
2. Elm
3. Cantabillae
4. Meeshla

NOTES ON PRONUNCIATION:

The Irish or Gaelic language, in general, carries a deeper vibration with it than English (a composite language of many different languages). The Gaelic language (found also in Scotland, Wales, Cornwall/Devonshire, the Isle of Man and Brittany) contributed much to the languages of Europe as the Celts made their way from India to their present-day homes. It's a very ancient language and similarities have been found in Galicia in Northwest Spain and in North Africa.

Sometimes in the healing of Earth or land, the vibration of the language and the sound of the music of the Ogham itself is needed. In my work with people who are not familiar with the sounds, there is sometimes a difficulty with pronunciation. In order to help people make the best use of these vibrations, the following guide may help:

beiṫ	Beh
luis	Luhss
feaRn	Fee-arn'
saille	Sall'yeh
nuin	Nuhn
uaṫe	Oo'hah
ðuiR	tDhuir
ṫinne	Chin'nah
coll	Call
queRṫ	Kerch

muin	Mwin
gort	Gorth
ngetal	Nedg'e–tal
straif	Ssthrayf
ruis	Ruhss
ailim	Ol'um
ohn	On
úr	Your
eaða	A
ioho	Oh'ho
coað	Hoe'ad
óir	Or
uilleanð	Ill'ah–and
pagos	Fadj'us
mór	Mor
conróis	Kon'roash
pís cumra	Peesh Hoov'rah
craoðliað corcra	Krayv'lee–ah Hoar'krah
faiðla rua	Fahv'lah Ru'ah
áirne	Arn'yeh
giúis	Gyoosh
saille šilte	Sall'yeh Heel'cheh
seiceamar	Sik'ah–mar
cnó capaill	K–noh' Kah'pull
reaðóig	Radg'oh–wig
leamán	Louw'in
cantabillae	Can–tab'i–lay
meeshla	Meesh'lah

Music of the Ogham

The Ogham sound has been known for millennia. The sound of Om (Aum) has been known and used by many other cultures since at least 5000 BC. The rishis (seers) of India developed a science called Mantra which traced the effects of sound on the body.

> All mantras derive their potency from Om because from this primordial energy-force all things come into expression. 'In the beginning was the Word, and the Word was with God, and the word was (is) God. All things were made by it, and without it was not anything made that was made.' (New Testament, *Gospel of St. John: 1:1* & 3). Also, Patanjali's *Yoga Sutras,* (1:27-29): 'The manifesting symbol (evidential aspect) of God is Om. One should meditate on this Word, contemplating and surrendering to it. Meditation on Om results in cosmic consciousness and the removal of all mental and physical obstacles to success on the on the spiritual path.'*

The following tune represents in sound the music of the Ogham. It is an ancient song whose composer is unknown. My own feeling is that this melody is part of the original creation: the Word.

● ●
* pg. 27. Davis, Roy Eugene. An Easy Guide to Meditation. Lakemont, Georgia: CSA Press, Publishers, 1995

These notes can be intoned with reverent intent as an aid to self-healing. Here are three different ways to work with these tones:

- pay attention to where and how each vibration is felt in the body – notice the difference in how you feel before and after;

- the tones can also raise the vibrations and bring harmony to any group or environment; and,

- this arrangement can be used with movement to release stress and tension, bringing about a feeling of harmony and peace.

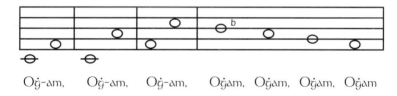

Oġ-am,   Oġ-am,   Oġ-am,   Oġam, Oġam, Oġam, Oġam

This chant should be sung (or played) very slowly and reverently. The word Oġam sounds like Aum (Om). The "g" with the buailte over it (ġ) is silent but carries a vibration with it that is deeper than the English equivalent in sound (Ogham).

Who will eat the kernel of the

nut must break the shell.

THE TREES AND THEIR LORE

GUIDE TO THE TREES

Within the following pages, you will find complete descriptions of the trees with their common and botanical names. Their Irish name is written first with the English translation afterwards. In some cases, there are illustrations of the trees (thanks to the Tree Council of Ireland). The Ogham symbol is given in each case, drawn in the appropriate colour for that tree.

Thirteen of the trees are associated with certain "months" of the year. Their approximate dates are shown (see section on the planets for a further explanation).

Next, is the section on the lore of the trees followed by an affirmation. Finally, in tabular order, are the characteristic, colour, gemstone, bird, month (where appropriate), element (Fire, Earth, Air, Water and Ether), planet, system and Ogham (for use with the cards). If you don't have a set of the cards*, you can read the Oghams as the positive and negative meanings of the tree.

· ·

*If you want to order a set of the cards (or oils and essences), an order form is provided in the back of the book.

Downy Birch

beiṫ / birch

novem6er 1 ⊤o 28

Common Names: White Birch, Beit Gheal/Silver Birch, Beit Chlúmhach/White or Downy Birch

BETULACEAE *Betula alba* Linnaeus; also *Betula pubescens* Ehrhart & *Betula pendula* Roth

DESCRIPTION: White bark all the way to the ground, although the Silver Birch develops dark, rugged cracks near the ground as it ages. The leaves are ovate to triangular about 2.5 inches (6 cm) long and 1.5 to 2 inches (5 cm) across. The White Birch leaf is pointed and has regular, single teeth and the Silver Birch is sharply pointed with coarse, double teeth. The leaves are dark green above and turn yellow in the autumn. The White or Downy Birch is so called because the shoots are downy or hairy as well as the veins underneath, especially when young. The Silver Birch leaves are carried on pendulous shoots which are slender and hairless. Flowers are catkins which break open when they are ripe. Birches will thrive in poor, wet, sandy soil and are a woodlands tree. Height reaches 80 to 100 feet (25 to 30 m).

Choosing Birch means that you are about to step out of the undergrowth. However, before setting off on a journey, it is best to check out the baggage and leave behind what you don't need. Old modes of thinking and negative influences need to be left behind. In starting out on your spiritual journey, keep this tree in mind as it grows up from and out of the undergrowth. If you are in the negative state of mind of this Ogham, you need to understand the purpose of your journey. You need to perhaps clear away old problems and cut ties with the past. It is difficult to put the right foot forward if the left foot is chained to the past.

Since Birch is about new beginnings, it is note-worthy that it was the Birch that was used in "birchings." The idea was that the old devils could be beaten out of the individual thus helping him/her to make a new start. Ruled by Venus;, Birch searches for beauty and is known as the Lady of the Forest. Birch is a commoner of the wood.

Silver Birch

Affirmation: I move forward with ease and grace.

Characteristic: Expansion
Colour: Infra Red
Gem Stone: Blue Sapphire
Bird: Robin

Month:	November 1 to 28– First Month of the Celtic Year
Element:	Ether
Planet:	Venus and Jupiter
System:	Muscular
Ogham:	UPRIGHT: By stepping out of the crowd and cleansing, you make a new beginning.
	REVERSED: You need to understand the purpose of your journey and focus on your goal.

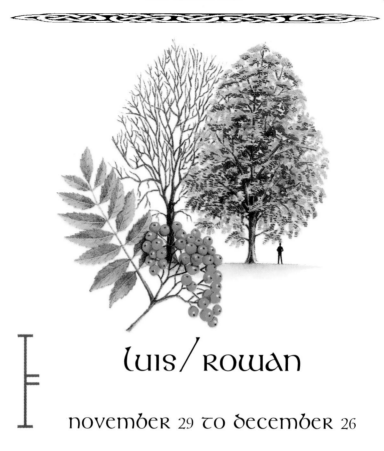

luıs / ROWAN

november 29 to december 26

Common Names: Rowan, Mountain Ash, Witchin, Wiggin Tree, Quicken and Caorthann

ROSACEAE *Sorbus aucuparia* Linnaeus

> DESCRIPTION: Rowan bark is smooth and grey. Its leaves (up to 8 inches/20 cm) have as many as seven pairs of smaller leaflets (up to 2.5 inches/6 cm) down the central stem with a single one on the end. There are no stems between the central

stalk and the leaflets. The smooth, dark green leaflets taper to a point and have sharp teeth. The undersides of the leaves are blue-green or grey with fine, cottony down underneath, especially when young. They turn yellow, red and even pink in the autumn. Rowan is most easily identified in the late spring with its huge clusters of small, creamy white flowers up to 6 inches (15 cm) across and, in the autumn, when the flowers have turned into heavy, pendulous clusters of bright red berries well loved by the birds. Rowans can be found in many locations from urban to woodlands, mountains and moorlands. They favor a moist, acid soil. Height to 50 feet (15 cm).

The Rowan or Mountain Ash grows higher up the mountain than any other tree. Ruled by Mars, the Rowan on the landscape is like a sentinel, protective and custodial. If you feel disturbed by destructive forces, find a Rowan tree and make friends with it. By planting a Rowan close to where you live, you are creating an ally both for yourself and others. Known in some places as the whispering tree, if you listen, it may share secrets with you. The Rowan (a commoner of the wood) was one of the sacred trees of the Ancients who understood its medicine.

On the spiritual path, we can be naive and trust everything and everybody. This tree represents discernment along the Way. The choosing of this oil/essence helps with psychic protection and helps you to discern between those who are act-

ing out of the best motives – for the greatest, highest good – and those whose motives are not pure. Rowan is the tree of good judgment. Within this Ogham is learning the lesson of becoming street wise. If you are not discerning enough, you need to use your own instincts to help you.

AFFIRMATION: I am protected and indestructible. Come what may, I am loved. I accept the sweetness and abundance of Life and acknowledge my gifts.

Characteristic:	Protection
Colour:	Indigo
Gem Stone:	Snow Quartz
Bird:	Wren
Month:	November 29 to December 26 – Second Month of the Celtic Year
Planet:	Jupiter and Mars
Balancer	
Ogham:	UPRIGHT: You are protected against destructive forces and have control of the senses.
	REVERSED: You are not discerning enough.

fearn/alder

december 27 to january 22

Common Names: Alder, Irish Mahogany, Fern, Fearnóg

Betalaceae *Alnus glutinosa* (Linnaeus) Gaertner

Description: The fissured bark is dark grey to brown-black. The heavy, leathery leaves (4 inches/10 cm long and 3 inches/7.5 cm across) are egg-shaped

with fine teeth and raised veins. The slightly sticky leaves are smooth and dark green above with tufts of soft grey down on the underside, especially when newly opened. Alder flowers in catkins resulting in small (.75 inches/2 cm), hard, woody, cone-like fruits. Alders are likely to be found near rivers. Height to 80 feet (25 m).

Alder (another commoner of the wood) is the tree which tells us that we have all come with our own special Book written in the stars. Through non-acceptance of our destiny and an unwillingness to open the Book, we become angry, blame ourselves and others and lack energy and joy. Within this Ogham, we learn about spiritual protection in disputes, an acceptance of ourselves and we learn to forgive both ourselves and others.

If you are having a dispute with a neighbour, plant Alder. Ruled by Venus, this tree will help restore harmony and turn anger to beauty. Its profusion of foliage speaks of its giving and generosity.

AFFIRMATION: I move forward with ease and grace.

Characteristic:	Expression
Colour:	Red
Gem Stone:	Lapis Lazuli
Bird:	Raven
Month:	December 27 to January 22 – Third Month of

	the Celtic Year
Element:	Fire
Planet:	Mercury, Venus and Mars
System:	Muscular

Ogham: UPRIGHT: By forgiving yourself and others and accepting your destiny, you are free flowing and have earned protection in disputes.

REVERSED: You need to forgive yourself and others and become more aware of the need for protection when in conflict.

saille/willow

JANUARY 23 TO FEBRUARY 19

Common Names: Willow, White Willow, Saileach Bhán

SALICACEAE *Salix Alba* Linnaeus

DESCRIPTION: A thick grey-brown trunk with deeply fissured, rugged bark, large branches and multitudes of smooth, slender shoots. The leaves are tapering and pointed on both ends (4 inches/10 cm long and 5/8 inches/1.5 cm across). The young

leaves are silvery with silky grey down. As they age, they become green on top and greyish underneath. Although the leaves look smooth, there are tiny teeth all the way around. The catkin flowers start out as small, egg-shaped buds with soft, fuzzy heads commonly called pussy willows or pussy buds. The fruit is a small, green capsule which releases fluffy, white seeds. Preferred habitat is along the rivers and water-meadows. Height to 80 feet (25 m).

The Willow is water loving and grows for preference in low lying areas. The Willow (a commoner of the wood) bends with the breeze and so teaches us that, to go with the flow of the Spiritual Path, will keep us pliable like the potter's clay. If we find it difficult to give birth to new ideas, we could become stiff in ourselves and so develop damp diseases and become rigid in our thinking. If we have the male and female well balanced within ourselves, we can truly enjoy the gift of creation. This Ogham oil/essence is very helpful for men who are becoming more in tune with the feminine aspects of themselves and for women who are denying their feminine aspects.

Ruled by the Moon, Willow is one of trees which tells us about the emotional body. Making the connection between water and the Moon will help us resolve our emotional baggage.

AFFIRMATION: I release that which no longer serves me. I am at one with my environment.

Characteristic:	Empathy
Colour:	Silver
Gem Stone:	Silver
Bird:	Thrush
Month:	January 23 to February 19 – Fourth Month of the Celtic Year
Element:	Water
Planet:	Moon
System:	Lymphatic
Ogham:	UPRIGHT: You are working with your emotional and Lunar rhythms to balance the male and female aspects of yourself.
	REVERSED: Your emotional and intuitive bodies are out of balance. You need to develop your creativity.

nuin/ash

february 20 to march 18

Common Names: Ash, Fuinseog and Uinnius

OLEACEAE *Fraxinus excelsior* Linnaeus

DESCRIPTION: Very straight trunk is pale grey and very smooth when young, cracking into irregular, upright fissures as it ages. The wood is used is making hurley sticks for the uniquely Irish game of hurling. A unique feature of the Ash is the way the twigs end in a stout, pale grey or yellow, slightly flattened

tip with fat, blackish buds at the end and around the sides. Four to eleven pairs of lance-shaped, taper-pointed leaflets (4 inches/10 cm long by 1.25 inches/3 cm wide) make up the leaf (12 inches/30 cm) of the Ash. There is a single leaf at the end. The leaflets are sharply pointed and have short stalks. Ash flowers sprout from the black buds in tiny, purple clusters and have no petals. The fruit called "keys" or "spinners" is winged and hangs in heavy dense clusters often remaining on the tree long after the leaves have dropped. Ash likes riverlands and moist woodlands with bare ground underneath. Height to 130 feet (40 m).

Along the Spiritual Path, we may need different keys to open the doors as we come to them. It is sometimes difficult to find the key. The keys of the Ash open the door to the sweetness of knowing that we are part of the whole. This knowing is a release from the separation that we feel from our own self-imposed introversion. Through the Ogham, we learn awareness of self in the bigger picture of the whole. If, like the Ash, our roots become sour and, if we fail to become like the Swallow which is a bird of perpetual motion, we could become stuck on the wheel of life building up bitterness and resentment from denial.

In the hierarchical order of trees, the Ash (which is ruled by the Sun) takes its place as an important tree of initiation. Through Ash (a noble of the wood), we may earn a rite of passage to the Other World and other dimensions. The Ash was

also known as a magical healer.

There is a very old tradition, in some places, that as a funeral passed by a particular Ash, the cortege stopped and the corpse was laid to rest for a few moments. My interpretation of this particular custom is that the "old" people recognized the Ash as a door opener to the greater whole. This gesture was meant to placate the Angel of the Ash so that the door might be opened for the soul who had just passed on.

Affirmation: I breathe Life easily. I speak my truth. I am protected. I am at one with my environment.

Characteristic:	Universal Truth
Colour:	Blue
Gem Stone:	Orange Carnelian
Bird:	Swallow
Month:	February 20 to March 18 – Fifth Month of the Celtic Year
Element:	Earth
Planet:	Sun, Mercury and Neptune
System:	Respiratory
Ogham:	Upright: You are aware of the part you play in the greater cosmic picture.

REVERSED: You have a tendency to introversion. You need to connect yourself to the greater Whole.

uate/hawthorn

march 19 to april 14

Common Names: Hawthorn, Whitethorn, May Tree, Skeaghbush, Sceach Gheal, Caorthann

ROSACEAE *Crataegus monogyna* Jacquin

DESCRIPTION: Small, dark grey to orange-brown trunk with rough and cracking bark which may be twisted like a rope. The deeply cut, pointed and toothed lobes of the leaves (2 inches/5 cm long and wide) are like blunt fingers with one to three lobes on

each side. Hawthorn leaves are glossy and dark green above, a paler underside having hairs on the leaf veins. Fairly large, creamy-white or pink flowers (5/8 inches/1.5 cm) have pink anthers and are borne in clusters in the late spring. Crimson, oval-shaped fruit with a single stone stays on the trees after the leaves have fallen and are very popular with the Birds. Hawthorn is found in woodlands, hedgerows and thickets. Height to 33 feet (10 m).

Ruled by Mars, Hawthorn carries with it many folk tales and anecdotes. Fairy Folk, it is said, live by the Hawthorn and Blackthorn. Hawthorn (a commoner of the wood) once marked the Way of the Pilgrimage which was also the ley line. Hawthorn is a cleanser of ley lines and landscapes, generally.

There is an old custom that Hawthorn would sometimes be planted near the place where an accident happened. I see this as meaning that both the soul and the place could be cleansed of the negative vibrations caused by the accident (or that caused the accident in the first place?).

In olden times, when a person died, their body was washed with water and hay. Then, the hay and the water which had been used were put under the Hawthorn bush.

As reclamation of the land has occurred, ditches have been done away with and Hawthorns have

gone with the ditches. If you are wondering how you could help Mother Nature, you could pick haws (the fruit of the Hawthorn) and plant them. It will take two years for them to re-appear as tiny plants.

Hawthorn is very feminine in its philosophy. It is the crone of the trees – Macha. The white of the Hawthorn flowers tells us of its cleansing ability. It represents a cleansing and breaking down of old structures and a clearing away of the un-wanted and outworn. If we don't let go of the old, we could become like the branches of the hawthorn, twisted and thorny. It is the tree which asks us to face up to the reality that as we progress on the Path, we may need to discard that which has already served its purpose.

If we are in the negative state of the philosophy of this tree, we could be holding on to the clut-ter. We may need to unload so that we can take fresh baggage on board. It may take time to un-load, so it is best not to go forward too quickly.

Affirmation: I release that which no longer serves me. I am at one with my environment.

Characteristic:	Cleansing
Colour:	Orange
Gem Stone:	Amethyst
Bird:	Whitethroat

Month:	March 19 to April 14 – Sixth Month of the Celtic Year
Element:	Ether
Planet:	Moon and Mars
System:	Lymphatic
Ogham:	UPRIGHT: By holding back and taking time to cleanse, it is possible to prepare for a new phase.
	REVERSED: You are trying to go forward too quickly.

ᗞuir/oak

april 15 ᴄo may 12

Common Names: Sessile Oak/Dair Neamh-ghasánach, Turkey Oak/Searbhdhair, Pendunculate Oak/Dair Choiteann, Dair Ghaelach

FAGACEAE *Quercus petraea* (Mattuschka) Lieblein

DESCRIPTION: Heavy, thick trunk, wide and spreading at the ground level with rough, dark grey or brown bark in vertical ridges and huge branches. Oak leaves (4.25 inches/ 12 cm long and 3 inches/7.5 cm wide) are elliptical or feather-shaped with smooth, rounded lobes or fingers. The leaves are glossy, dark green and somewhat leathery with a prominent central vein and slightly hairy underneath. The catkin flowers turn into acorns in the fall. Favorite habitat is the woodlands. Height to 130 feet (40 m).

The Oak (a noble of the wood) takes 300 years to come to maturity and grow, 300 years being and 300 years dying. Its roots go as deep into the Earth as its branches go up to Heaven. The leaves of the Oak are very fine and etheric for such a strong tree. The Oak talks to us of strengthening our roots in the Earth, as well as strengthening ourselves in Heaven. If we live too much in Heaven, we might be no earthly good. If we live too much in Earth, we might be no Heavenly good.

The great mystery of life is to emulate the Oak and achieve a balance between Heaven and Earth. When we have acquired our balance, we have overcome ourselves. The Ogham of the Oak teaches us to bring into the Earth the Mysteries and gifts we have spiritually attained while at the same time retaining our balance. Of all the trees, the Oak represents true balance and fights for this all the time.

The month of May is traditionally the month of Mary, the month when the Prayer of Mary (the Rosary) is said. The Rosary represents the story of our passageway in time. Just as the Rosary opens doors to the mysteries of life and death, so too does the Oak open doors to the same mysteries.

The Oak is also associated with the Yule log. In Druidic times, all household fires were put out. The Druids created the first fire of the season with their Yule log. Fire was then passed to the households by way of torches lit from the sacred fire.

AFFIRMATION: I let go of old patterns and absorb Life's lessons with wisdom and joy.

Characteristic:	Endurance
Colour:	Ultra Violet
Gem Stone:	Tiger's Eye (Golden Brown)
Bird:	Nightingale
Month:	April 15 to May 12 – Seventh Month of the Celtic Year
Element:	Air
Planet:	Jupiter and Venus
System:	Digestive

Ogham:

UPRIGHT: The strength and security of the Oak help lead you to the doors of your initiations along the Path.

REVERSED: You need to focus on what is required in the areas of protection and balance to go forward.

ꚗinne/holly

mꙗy 13 ꚗo june 9

Common Names: Holly, Common Holly, Holm Tree, Cuileann

AQUIFOLIACEAE *Ilex aquifolium* Linnaeus

DESCRIPTION: Pale grey bark, slender, smooth trunk with many branches near the ground. Holly leaves are a dark, glossy green and vary in shape from an ellipse to egg-shaped (up to 4 inches/10 cm long

by 2 inches/5 cm wide). Lower leaves are very prickly with sharp spines and wavy edges. Upper leaves are generally spineless. Usually male and female flowers grow in clusters on separate trees and are small, white and fragrant. The resulting dense clusters of red berries are greatly loved by the birds who will often strip the Holly of berries by Christmas time. Holly especially likes Beech and Oak woodlands. Height to 65 feet (20 m).

Holly is the Christ tree. At Christmas, we bring in the Holly and the Ivy as a reminder to banish resentment and anger and to allow love to flow. Holly has developed its spiritual arguments very well. Its leaves are very strong in winter and, if you come too close to the Holly with wrong ideas, you might get your fingers pricked.

The Holly (a noble of the wood) can withstand anything and is safe no matter what is directed at it. Its strength in the forest is an inspiration to other trees because it is a wonderful catalyst. The Holly stands apart, tall and straight. It also represents the Prophet in his/her own land.

There is an Irish tradition that Holly should always be treated with respect and never abused. There is also a belief that, if Holly trees are planted near a house where there are female children, the girls will never marry or, if they do marry, will never have children of their own. My understanding of this story is that because Holly

is the Christ tree, the girls in the house have chosen to be creative in a very different and special way. They have chosen to become Holly trees themselves. Since trees were once walking people, Holly as a walking person is very strong spiritually (or has that potential).

The Holly Ogham teaches us that, even though we may feel ostracised for the position we have taken up, we are able to withstand the storm. And, without losing our centre, we are able to bring forth the Gold that has been burnished by the fire. Gold is the gift of wholesomeness that comes as a result of having been through the flames, cleansing the dross.

If you are in the negative state of the philosophy of this tree, you could be out of balance and lack direction in your struggle. You may need to identify your position more clearly in order to become equipped to deal with your situation. This oil/essence is good to use before meditation, for use by healers and those involved in giving Spiritual direction.

The song of the Lark (the bird associated with Holly) is very clear and it soars high above other birds in the sky to sing its song. If you can soar above the din and noise, your position will become clearer.

AFFIRMATION: I am supported in life.

Characteristic:	Strength
Colour:	Gold
Gem Stone:	Ruby
Bird:	Lark
Month:	May 13 to June 9 – Eighth Month of the Celtic Year
Element:	Fire
Planet:	Mars, Saturn and Uranus
System:	Skeletal
Ogham:	UPRIGHT: Your well-founded strong, spiritual arguments are an inspiration to others. You are a leader in the fight.
	REVERSED: You are lacking direction and balance. You need these attributes to succeed.

coll/hazel

june 10 to july 7

Common Names: Hazel, Coll, Cobnut

BETULACEAE *Corylus avellana* Linnaeus

DESCRIPTION: Grey bark on a straight, thick trunk with many long arching branches and spreading roots. Leaves (up to 4 inches/10 cm) are dark-green, nearly round with irregular, almost jagged, toothed edges which come to a sharp point and are hairy, especially topside. Flowers are yellow catkins which

mature into clusters of 1 to 4 nuts, called cobs, that turn brown when they are ripe. While still green, they are partially surrounded by conspicuous bracts. The nuts are edible. Favored habitat is in hedgerows, woodlands and scrub land. Height to 33 feet (10 m).

The Hazel (a noble of the wood) was held by the Celts in high regard. The salmon and the hazel in Irish legend are associated with knowledge. In the River Boyne, which flows by Newgrange, the salmon swam under the overhanging Hazel. From the Hazel, fell the nine poetic nuts of wisdom. These were eaten by the salmon. Thus the knowledge in the Hazel nuts was absorbed. The last name of Fionn, who later ate the salmon of wisdom, was Mac Coll or Son of Hazel.

Gifts of the Spirit are often blocked within us through denial or a refusal to own them and make them our own. The faculty of Intuition, which leads straight to the source, is a wonderful capability. The Ogham oil/essence of Coll helps bring forth this – and other – blocked spiritual talents. By developing our intuition, the possibilities for us are limitless as we pull back the veils one at a time.

Ruled by Mercury, this oil/essence is very good for people who are developing their own and helping others to develop their intuitive skills and their listening abilities. The Hazel helps us to get in

touch with and develop intuition furthering our evolution.

Green is the colour associated with this oil and essence. The gemstone remedy is Emerald. Part of the personality of green reflects the evolving environment both external and internal. Hazel twigs, for example, are used in divining for water.

AFFIRMATION: I release that which no longer serves me. I am at one with my environment.

Characteristic:	Intuition and Communication
Colour:	Green
Gem Stone:	Emerald
Bird:	Kingfisher
Month:	June 10 to July 7 – Ninth Month of the Celtic Year
Element:	Water
Planet:	Moon and Mercury
System:	Lymphatic
Ogham:	UPRIGHT: By developing your intuition, the possibilities for you are limitless. Communicating directly with the source of your Self gives birth

to the next step in your evolution.

REVERSED: By denying your intuition, you are denying your gifts. Focus on your communication skills and your inner knowing.

quert/apple

Common Names: Apple, Crab Apple, Crann Fia-úll

ROSACEAE *Malus sylvestris* Miller

DESCRIPTION: Bark is greyish-brown, scaly and fissured. The tree is often found in a shrub-like form with reddish-brown twigs. Leaves are oval or rounded, especially at the base, with serrated edges. Wooliness upon first sprouting disappears as the leaves are fully formed. They have a characteristic stubby stalk about half the length of the leaf. Flowers are white with pink edges or undersides, have five petals and grow in clusters. The yellowish-green apple has some red areas, is sour and juicy. Habitat: mostly hedgerows and woodlands. Height to 33 feet (10 m).

Armagh is known as the orchard of Ireland. In an orchard, there are many apples to choose from, each apple looking equally good and inviting. As in the orchard, this Ogham is about making choices. There can be a lot of confusion when we have choices to make especially if all the choices are equally inviting. At Halloween, we try to bite the apples but we can only bite one apple at a time. In trying to keep all our options open, our energies could become very scattered. The Gem Stone remedy Obsidian is for helping us when our energies are scattered. We are faced

all the time with choices and we can become unbalanced from not actually making the choice.

The Corncrake of this Ogham is interesting. In a field, its song seems to come from everywhere. You can never tell where the Corncrake is so your energies could become very scattered looking for him.

This Ogham oil/essence is very good for people who feel they want to keep their options open. It will help where there is confusion and imbalance from the panic of not being able to choose.

The black colour of this Ogham represents the transformation of the black of the Earth to the heavenly black of the Caduceus. The Apple is a noble of the wood.

AFFIRMATION: I am at one with and trust the pulse of Life. I accept the sweetness and abundance of Life and acknowledge my gifts.

Characteristic:	Decisiveness
Colour:	Black
Gem Stone:	Obsidian
Bird:	Corncrake
Element:	Earth
Planet:	Mercury, Mars and Saturn
System:	Nervous

Ogham:

UPRIGHT: Your commit-
ment to your own trans-
formation and beauty
helps you make bal-
anced choices.

REVERSED: Your energies
are scattered. You need
to choose carefully.

muin/vine

july 8 to august 6

Common Names: Vine, Grape Vine

VITACEAE *Vitis vinifera*

> DESCRIPTION: Woody climber. Leaves are deeply lobed and are scarlet in the autumn. Fruit is purplish black, sweet and edible. Height/length up to 50 feet (15.25 m).

The vine in the Ogham alphabet is very healing. The colour of the Red wine of the Eucharist reminds us of the life force of Christ – the Heart Beat of the Universe. In the Eucharist and the Ogham of the Vine is the possibility of reaping the harvest of our labours. By opening up our senses to the influx of love and energy available to us, we can become our true selves and so learn to trust what we receive. By allowing instinct to guide us, we can develop an unshakable faith and trust.

The Ogham oil/essence of Muin helps us to unwind as people do after gathering the harvest. It is very good for helping with the flowering of the fruits of the senses in the knowing that the abun-

dance of the Universe supports. Muin is good for balancing and for helping to open us up to the love which we deserve.

AFFIRMATION: I allow love to flow freely through me.

Characteristic:	Nourishment
Colour:	Green
Gem Stone:	Rose Quartz
Bird:	Water-Hen
Month:	July 8 to August 6 – Tenth Month of the Celtic Year
Element:	Ether
Planet:	Sun and Venus
System:	Circulatory
Ogham:	UPRIGHT: Nourishment, love and the gift of prophecy come to you as the harvest of your labours.
	REVERSED: You need to unwind and trust your feelings.

GORT/ IVY

AUGUST 7 TO SEPTEMBER 4

Common Names: Ivy, Common Ivy, English Ivy

ARALIACEAE *Hedera helix*

> DESCRIPTION: Self-branching climber. Leaves range from small (1 inch/2 cm square or less) up to 2 inches/5 cm or more. They are usually deeply lobed but are variable in shape and can sometimes be triangular, sometimes variegated. They are usually evergreen. Height/length varies depending on the height of the host tree.

The Ivy as it grows wanders through many other plants, in and around them, searching for its path. The soul on its path is like the Ivy spiralling through the labyrinth in its search for itself. There can be no soul growth without going into the heart. The doctrine of Signatures teaches us that everything has a memory of itself (how else does the acorn know to grow into an Oak?). When we learn to look at plants, we can tell what their purpose is. Ground Ivy has the shape of a heart on its leaf. The Ivy in its negative can choke what is coming out of its heart and, in this way, loses sight of the real goal of its journey. The Ogham

of Gort teaches us to act unselfishly and with pure motives.

This oil/essence is good for people who find it difficult to express unconditional love, who are jealous of others or who cannot give people space in a relationship. Gort is helpful for people who are trying to control others or who are themselves being controlled. It helps people pull away the tendrils so that they can become free spirits. This gives the freedom to explore the meaning of "Know Thyself."

AFFIRMATION: I breathe Life easily. I speak my truth. I am protected. I am at one with my environment.

Characteristic:	Freedom
Colour:	Blue
Gem Stone:	Pearl
Bird:	Starling
Month:	August 7 to September 4 – Eleventh Month of the Celtic Year
Element:	Air
Planet:	Venus, Uranus and Pluto
System:	Respiratory & Skin
Ogham:	UPRIGHT: The spiral of Newgrange creates for you the image of the

inner spiral and the search for self.

REVERSED: Ivy can choke. You need to act with unconditional love and out of pure motives.

ngetal/reed

september 5 to october 1

Common Names: Reed, Sea Rush

JUNCACAEAE *Juncus maritimus* Lam.

> DESCRIPTION: Commonly found as a green, tubular "leaf" about 3 to 6 feet (100 to 200 cm) long. Has feathery brown seed tufts and grows in the shallow waters of salt marshes and coastal wetlands.

The Reed grows tall and straight and, as the breeze blows, the Reed bends with the wind. The Reed bends but does not break. As they are blown by the wind, the Reeds speak to each other, as if telling each other their story. Once the Reed has discovered that it won't break, it is no longer afraid of bending.

The Ogham of the Reed teaches us that the trials and tribulations that we face on the spiritual path are all leading us somewhere. If we move in the flow of the energy as it bends us, we do indeed become the "willing servant" as John puts it. This Ogham teaches us to work with conviction from the centre of ourselves and from the power within.

AFFIRMATION: I am indestructible. Come what may, I am loved.

Characteristic:	Flexibility
Colour:	White
Gem Stone:	Bloodstone
Bird:	Goldfinch
Month:	September 5 to October 1 – Twelfth Month of the Celtic Year
Element:	Fire
Planet:	Venus and Moon
Balancer	
Ogham:	UPRIGHT: Your commitment to being a willing servant empowers you to direct action and yet still bend with the wind.
	REVERSED: To prepare yourself for the next part of your journey, you need to polish up your skills.

 straif/blackthorn

Common Names: Blackthorn, Sloe

ROSACEAE *Prunus spinosa*

> DESCRIPTION: Shrub-like with dark, thorny bark often found in hedgerows. In a grove, it may form a canopy and send out sucker roots. Leaf is toothed, dark-green, elliptical and comes to a point at both ends. It has prominent veins and a leathery appearance. Dense clouds of white flowers with gold tipped anthers cover the tree before the leaves appear. The resulting fruits look like plums and are dark purple but are bitter. Height to 16 feet (5 m).

The Blackthorn has very strong vicious thorns on its branches. This characteristic gives us a clue to its personality. It is not easy to get through a Blackthorn hedge. To get through the Blackthorn hedge is to pass quite a test, especially when you have no choice.

This Ogham is about learning lessons when there is no choice. Blackthorn (lower division of the wood) doesn't give us any choice. Once through the Blackthorn, however, there comes a flowering. When there is no choice, it is best to go with the flow, giving way to events. Accepting your situation may be difficult but it will help you emerge into a new fulfilling phase. If you persist

with a negative viewpoint, life could be difficult.

As a note: the pronunciation of Straif is very close the English word "Strife" which is evocative of the feeling of this Ogham.

AFFIRMATION: I am supported in Life.

Characteristic:	Surrender
Colour:	Violet
Gem Stone:	Moonstone
Bird:	Cuckoo
Element:	Water
Planet:	Mars, Saturn and Neptune
System:	Skeletal

Ogham: UPRIGHT: Because you accept that there is no choice in your situation, unpleasant though it may be, you emerge into a new, more fulfilling phase.

REVERSED: Accepting that what will be may be difficult. You are persisting with a negative viewpoint.

RUIS / eLòeR

octobeR 2 to 31 — samain

Common Names: Elder, Bour-tree, Trom

CAPRIFOLIACEAE *Sambucus nigra* Linnaeus

> DESCRIPTION: The trunk is usually fairly small and may divide close to the ground so that it looks shrub-like. The bark is grey or brown (shading towards tan) with many deep furrows especially when older. Compound leaves have two to three pairs of leaflets with a single one at the end. Leaves are pale green, round to oval, toothed and come to a point (up to 3.5 inches/9 cm). The many, small white flowers form clusters (like a posy) which are upright, flat and about 4 to 8 inches across (10 to 20 cm). The small black fruits hang in clusters on red stalks. Both the flowers and the fruits are used to make wine. Habitat: hedgerows, abandoned farms, easily seeded almost anywhere by birds. Height to 33 feet (10 m) (rarely).

In the Ogham Calendar, the 13th month is ruled by the Elder (lower division of the wood). Samhain is pronounced "sow'in." Because it is the last month of the year, our minds automatically turn to beginnings and endings. We are reminded by the Elder of regeneration, of leaving behind the old and giving birth to the new. Giving birth

should be a joyful experience when we have learned to breathe. The lessons must be learned and the wheel turns constantly through life, death and rebirth.

The Elder re-grows damaged branches very easily. The Ogham of the Elder teaches us that, if the lesson we have had to learn has been difficult for us, we can renew and regenerate ourselves through this oil/essence.

The Blackbird is a bird of song. The Irish Dance called the Blackbird is a joy to watch as the steps change with the rhythm. Remembering to move with the flow brings a rhythm to our lives as we dance to the song of the Blackbird.

This oil/essence is good for people who are moving from one stage of development to another and are finding the change traumatic. It also cleanses in this situation.

AFFIRMATION: I breathe Life easily. I speak my truth. I am protected. I am at one with my environment.

Characteristic:	Change
Colour:	Orange
Gem Stone:	Turquoise
Bird:	Blackbird
Month:	October 2 to 31 (Samhain) – Thirteenth

	Month of the Celtic Year
Element:	Earth
Planet:	Pluto and Venus
System:	Respiratory and Skin

Ogham:

U<small>PRIGHT</small>: The end in the beginning and the beginning in the end. The turnings of the triple spiral: life, death and rebirth.

R<small>EVERSED</small>: By resisting you can make life difficult. The circle will turn anyway.

ailim/silver fir

Common Names: Silver Fir, European Silver Fir

PINACEAE *Abies alba* Miller

DESCRIPTION: Brownish-grey bark is smooth and greyish-silver in its youth, becoming deeply cracked and browner with age. The dark green leaves are flat, round-tipped, have a central furrow, two silvery lines down the undersides and grow singly like bristles on the branch. The flowers are male and the cones (4 to 8 inches/10 to 20 cm) are female. The cones stand upright on the higher branches and form downward pointing bracts giving it a rather untidy or hairy appearance. Habitat: mountainsides and forest lands. Height to 165 feet (50 m).

The Silver Fir (noble of the wood), with its tall, graceful, swan-like elegance, is able to see over long distances. This tree speaks of the integration of masculine and feminine. It speaks of the power of the Red and Violet which make Magenta. It teaches us of the power of the feminine which, when discovered, leads to a vision of the needs of humanity. This oil is truly the healers' oil: for the people of vision and for those developing clairvoyance.

The bird of the Ailim is the Swan — the bird of grace and beauty. With this Ogham, we are reminded of the story of the children of Lir (Light) who were turned into swans and banished for 900 years. Symbolically, the light went out and darkness reigned. With faith, the light will return. With vision, the darkness and light can be balanced.

AFFIRMATION: I am balanced between Spirit and matter.

Characteristic:	Vision
Colour:	Magenta
Gem Stone:	Olivine
Bird:	Swan
Element:	Ether
Planet:	Jupiter
System:	Glandular
Ogham:	UPRIGHT: Your insight has given you an overview of your own and others' Paths.
	REVERSED: Your vision is clouded. You need to stand aside and review your situation.

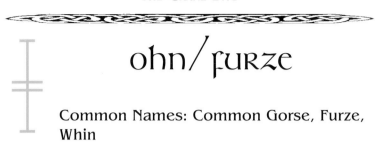

ohn/ furze

Common Names: Common Gorse, Furze, Whin

LEGUMINOSAE *Ulex europaeus*

DESCRIPTION: Evergreen shrub, often with sharp spines. The three common names indicate slight variations on a theme. They all have golden pea-like flowers which are often fragrant, smelling of coconut. The Whin version has slightly greyish green leaves. All versions have small thin leaves although the Gorse leaves may be quite long and almost needle-like. They thrive on the moorlands. Height to 6 feet (2 m).

The very colour of the Furze is Gold and this gives us an insight into this Ogham. To become golden, we need to gather together a lot of bits and pieces, information and knowledge and make it our own. Our minds could be very active doing this so Furze (bush of the woods) helps very much on the mental plane.

Different energies need to be brought together from different sources. If the gathering together isn't done, we might be found wanting and find ourselves unable to pass on to the next stage of our journey. So, the Furze teaches us to bring together those things which are of value to us.

The bird of the Furze is the Magpie which is renowned for gathering.

AFFIRMATION: I accept the sweetness and abundance of Life and acknowledge my gifts. I am at one with and trust the pulse of Life.

Characteristic:	Hope
Colour:	Gold
Gem Stone:	Clear Topaz
Bird:	Magpie
Element:	Air
Planet:	Mars and the Sun
System:	Nervous
Ogham:	UPRIGHT: You are good at collecting like a magpie. Gathering together brings sunshine.
	REVERSED: More work needs to be done. The gathering together is not yet complete.

úr/heather

Common Names: Heather, Heath, Connemara Heath, Irish Heath

ERICACEAE *Daboecia cantabrica*, many varieties of *Erica* are also found

DESCRIPTION: Evergreen shrub with a spreading habit. Tiny, dark green leaves can look burnt in the winter. Irish Heather has larger, puffier, more upright flowers than *Erica* which are a magenta, rosy pink or white. Heather grows on the mountains and moorlands. Height: 18 inches (45 cm) to 3 feet (1 m).

The very fine delicate flowers of the Heather (bush of the woods) tell us that, even though it is found mostly on the mountain where it is exposed to the gales and the elements, it is a very sensitive plant. The mountain itself is able to withstand being buffeted by the elements but the Heather must feel the pain yet continue to grow in this fashion.

The Ogham of the heather teaches us that, if we are strong within ourselves, we can withstand anything. The spiritual strength that we need will be found with ourselves if we look for the healing and wholeness of the fire of the mountain. We must go within ourselves to find it.

Heather is good for those who have the child within wounded — good for the recluse, for those shutting themselves off from the world (the heather is very exposed on the mountain), for those feeling separation.

The bird of the heather is the Pheasant — what colour this bird has! The Pheasant can be an inspiration to those who need the spiritual colour of Violet to bring themselves back into balance.

AFFIRMATION: I am at one with and trust the pulse of Life.

Characteristic:	Simplicity
Colour:	Violet
Gem Stone:	Amethyst
Bird:	Pheasant
Element:	Fire
Planet:	Sun
System:	Nervous
Ogham:	UPRIGHT: Heather links you to the child within, to your simplicity and child-like essence.
	REVERSED: You need to look at the inner world of healing and wholeness.

 # eaða/white poplar

Common Names: Aspen, Asp, Quaking Esp, Crann Creathach, White Poplar, Abele Tree

SALICACEAE *Populus alba* (White Poplar); SALICACEAE *Populus tremula* Linnaeus (Aspen)

DESCRIPTION: Aspen and White Poplar are closely related trees with basically the same vibration. However, the appearance of each tree is distinct and easily identified so both will be compared and contrasted. The bark of both trees is white (or some-

times greenish-silver in the case of the Aspen). The White Poplar has larger areas of dark marks which become fissured bark. The slim, dark areas on the Aspen are horizontal with some dark vertical scarring as the tree ages and darkens to a grey color. Both trees sucker freely. The leaves of the White Poplar (3.5 inches/9 cm) are dark green on top and fuzzy or woolly white below, have three to five distinct lobes. The Aspen leaves are nearly round, coarsely toothed or wavy margins coming to a dainty point. Aspen leaf stalks are flattened and as long as the leaf (2.5 inches/6 cm) causing it to catch every wind with characteristic trembling and rustling. Both trees flower in catkins with male and female flowers on separate trees. The female flowers of both produce fluffy white or woolly seeds which are born on the wind. These trees prefer damp, riverside or meadowland sites, although the Aspen will be found in hedges, copses, moorlands, mountainsides while Poplars are often planted to form windbreaks. Height: White Poplar to 100 feet (30 m); Aspen to 65 feet (20 m).

On the calmest day in summer, the leaves of the Aspen shimmer on the tree. With the slightest puff of wind, the leaves rustle and shake. If we are afraid, we could shake like the Poplar (lower division of the wood). So, the White Poplar teaches us to overcome fear. It is the tree of courage. To have the courage to express ourselves and become the true blue, we must work out a lot of fear.

The person who has learned to overcome fear has faith and trust that is unshakable. Fear in

many situations is lack of faith and trust. Since our faith is often tested on the Spiritual Path, we may need a little help. The oil or essence of the White Poplar helps us overcome fear. A lot of our fears are triggered by memories that we carry with us.

The oil/essence of White Poplar is good for situations where, like the Aspen, the puff of wind frightens us. If we listen to the message on the wind, then there is no need to shake.

The bird associated with the Poplar and Aspen is the Sooty Black Swift. This bird shows his fear in a particular way. He doesn't have a song so he is, we could say, joyless — frightened to death.

AFFIRMATION: I accept with courage the Divine flow.

Characteristic:	Faith
Colour:	Royal Blue
Gem Stone:	Citrine
Bird:	Sooty Black Swift
Element:	Water
Planet:	Saturn and Mars
System:	Urinary
Ogham:	UPRIGHT: Tree of trust, Aspen gives you spiritual guidance and cour-

age through the still inner voice.

REVERSED: Your fears are shutting out the voice in the wind. You need to listen to your instincts.

ıoho / yew

Common Names: Yew, Common Yew, European Yew, Eó, tIúr Éireannach

TAXACEAE *Taxus baccata* Linnaeus "Fastigiata"

DESCRIPTION: Bark is reddish-brown, furrowed and comes off in flakes. The evergreen needles are short, awl-shaped, blackish-green (undersides paler), twisted and flattened with pointed ends. The flowers are inconspicuous, although the male flowers will spew out clouds of yellow pollen if they are

struck in the Spring. The fruit is red (infrequently yellow), cup-shaped (which partially encloses the seed). Yews can live 2000 years. Habitat: moorlands and downs, frequently planted in gardens and churchyards. Height to 65 feet (20 m).

Legend teaches us that the Yew grows a root into each corpse in the graveyards. Knowing the connection between death and birth tells us that the philosophy of the Yew teaches us about birth, death and regeneration. It talks to us of the flashback of the memory that gives us insight. We really can't move into the future until we have considered the past and healed it.

The Yew (noble of the wood) teaches us about the eternal turnings of the spiral which is ceaseless. Yew oil and essence help bring up the memories that are blocking us which, when healed, allow our wisdom to come through.

The Eagle in mysticism is a very important bird and John is often referred to as the Eagle. The Eagle is far-seeing and the Guardian or Keeper of the Gate, just like the Yew is the symbolic Keeper of the graveyards. With the Eagle's help, it is possible to look very far in all directions, thus forming a vision of all that is required to be taken from the past through the Gate and into the future for renewal and regeneration.

The Mother Yew of all Yews grows in a field near Florence Court in County Fermanagh, Northern Ireland.

AFFIRMATION: I am at one with my creative source.

Characteristic:	Renewal
Colour:	Orange
Gem Stone:	Turquoise
Bird:	Eagle
Element:	Earth
Planet:	Saturn and Pluto
System:	Reproductive
Ogham:	UPRIGHT: By rebirthing, you can renew spiritual strength and free past memories.
	REVERSED: You need to let go of the past to move into the future.

coad/grove

DESCRIPTION: Blend of many the trees that make up the naturally occurring Grove.

Of all the Ogham, Coad is the one which teaches us most about acceptance. To get to the point of acceptance, we need to be very balanced within ourselves. Coad asks us to balance the Heaven and Earth. To achieve this task, we may need to find a grove (either physically or through the oil/essence) where we can gather together the wisdom and knowledge of the trees. This brings us unity and clarity.

If we are in the negative frame of mind of this Ogham, we could be concentrating too narrowly on one or two aspects of our life. Thereby, we could be excluding so much more knowledge and wisdom that is available to us if only we could accept it.

The Owl is associated with Coad and, since the wisdom of the Owl is well known, he is a wonderful friend along the Path.

AFFIRMATION: I am indestructible. Come what may, I am loved.

Characteristic: Knowledge

Colour:	Green
Gem Stone:	Emerald
Bird:	Owl
Element:	Ether
Planet:	Uranus and Chiron
Balancer	

Ogham:	UPRIGHT: Finding a sacred place where all is linked in togetherness and unity bring clarity.
	REVERSED: You are concentrating too narrowly on one or two aspects of yourself to the exclusion of so much else.

óir / spinðle

Common Names: Spindle, Spindle Tree, Pegwood, Feoras

CELASTRACEAE *Euonymus eqropaeus* Linnaeus

DESCRIPTION: Bark is smooth and greyish-green. Although it can occur with a single trunk, it is more often seen with several main branches or independent trunks starting at or near the ground, giving it a shrub-like appearance. The leaves are bright green, pointed, finely toothed with prominent veins about 4 inches/10 cm long. They are narrow, oval to elliptical in shape and occur in opposite pairs. The greenish-white or pale yellow flowers have four petals and occur in stalked clusters of 3 to 8. They produce an unusual fruit with four chambered, cherry pink capsules which open like valves and enclose seeds which are encased in bright orange flesh (the "aril"). Spindles prefer scrublands, limestone and chalk regions. Height to 20 feet (6 m).

The fruit of the Spindle (lower division of the wood) reminds us of the four chambers of the heart. In order to open up the heart to the ultimate, Love demands a lot of discipline and hard work. The Ogham of the Spindle teaches us that happiness is gained, not as a right, but as a gift through this labour of love. The labour may demand that we live in the present, having left

the past behind and with no expectations of the future.

Mundane tasks can be a source of soul growth, particularly when done with love and intent. Through the mundane, we can come into the wisdom of the heart. This Ogham teaches us that all that is required is that we do our best. When we least expect it, there is a surprise in store for us.

Spindle Ogham oil/essence helps those who are finding it difficult to concentrate on the job in hand and those whose heart energies are blocked through an inability to discipline themselves.

AFFIRMATION: I allow love to flow freely through me.

Characteristic:	Love
Colour:	Golden Yellow
Gem Stone:	Amethyst
Bird:	House Martin
Element:	Air
Planet:	Sun and Venus
System:	Circulatory
Ogham:	UPRIGHT: You are doing your best with love, tirelessly.

REVERSED: You may not regard happiness as a right. It is a gift that has to be earned.

uilleand/

honeysuckle

Common Names: Honeysuckle, Woodbine

CAPRIFOLIACEAE *Lonicera periclymenum*

> DESCRIPTION: Deciduous climber with vigorous growth. Leaves are elliptical and pointed at both ends with a pale central rib and veins. The very fragrant flowers form in large clusters of creamy-white with pink or crimson tubes and buds. These plants are found mostly in hedgerows and along garden fences.

Honeysuckle is very sweet smelling. Within its perfume are hidden secrets. These secrets are there for the finding when the background clutter is cleared away.

The Ogham of the Honeysuckle helps us to clear away that which is restrictive to the soul's purpose. To carry Honeysuckle on the Path reminds us to keep our eye on our ultimate destiny and leads us eventually to the fertile Secrets of the soul. This Ogham encourages us not to doubt ourselves but to trust, knowing there are rewards in the secrets of the Honeysuckle.

AFFIRMATION: I allow love to flow freely through me. I accept the sweetness and abundance of Life and acknowledge my gifts.

Characteristic:	Centredness
Colour:	Indigo
Gem Stone:	Blue Sapphire
Bird:	Lapwing
Element:	Fire
Planet:	Sun and Neptune
System:	Circulatory
Ogham:	UPRIGHT: Finding the hidden secrets and discovering your gifts leads to an opening of the heart and connects you to your soul's purpose.
	REVERSED: You are finding it difficult to pick out your gifts in the background noise.

⻑pagos/beech

Common Names: Beech, Common Beech, Feá, Fáidhbhile

FAGACEAE *Fagus sylvatica* Linnaeus

DESCRIPTION: Bark is grey and smoothes on a massive trunk. The tree is well shaped with a huge spread providing dense shade. Leaves (4 inches/ 10 cm) start out light green and silky on the undersides, quickly becoming hairless (except on the main vein and leaf stalk), dark green and shiny until autumn when they turn a rich golden or reddish-brown. They are oval shaped and pointed. The edges are wavy at the vein end. The flowers are catkins producing the beech mast containing 2 (usually) glossy, brown, pyramidal shaped nuts.

These nuts are protected by a bristly exterior which splits into four parts to release them. Beeches are woodland trees and often are found in chalky and well-drained sandy regions. Height to 130 feet (40 m).

Beech is known as the Mother of the Forest. As she shelters the younger trees striving to survive, she shares with them her wisdom. To learn from past experiences is true wisdom. It is even wiser to learn from other people's wisdom. People, places and objects bring us this wisdom. If we can use this gift of other peoples' wisdom, we can learn the lessons of life in a joyful way.

The Beech holds a lot of memories and these can be easily taken out of the Earth through the wisdom of this tree. When we need to recall the wisdom of our own past, this Ogham oil/essence will help us. The Beech teaches us also to be real listeners — to what is not being said as well as to what is being said. The Beech can lead us to the Source of ourselves.

The bird of the Beech is the Crane. The Crane Cleric, Columcille, was known for his wisdom.

Affirmation: I let go of old patterns and absorb Life's lessons with wisdom and joy.

Characteristic: Tolerance
Colour: Orangish Brown

Gem Stone:	Tiger's Eye
Bird:	Crane
Element:	Earth
Planet:	Moon and Saturn
System:	Digestive

Ogham:

UPRIGHT: Learning from wisdom of the past through people, places and objects develops tolerance and joy.

REVERSED: You may need to listen to the voice of experience to avoid making mistakes.

mór/τhe sea

As rebirth is inevitable, with waters before and waters after, this Ogham teaches us about our hidden depths and resources. It teaches us about the roots from which we came, about the cauldron and the inevitability of going back to the Source.

The water used in this formula is taken from the Holy Well of Brigid of Faughart near Dundalk. This well is very sacred and cleansing. The well is situated on a hill within the original Temple of Brigid where there are Yew trees (another symbol of rebirth).

The mountains, which stretch across the border of North and South of Ireland, protect and safeguard Brigid as she waits for us. Beside her well grows a Wild Rose. To the North are the Mountains of Mourne. To the South is a view of Tara and the Hill of Slane.

This place of peace is very feminine and welcoming. People come here and leave something belonging to themselves — usually pieces of cloth which they tie to the trees — as a symbol of giving something of themselves as they seek hearing. There is a stone in this Temple with a "cut" in it which the moon shines into only once every

three years. This cycle reminds us of the Triple Spiral and the Triple Goddess.

As we cleanse in the waters of the well, we are reminded of several things: of the womb, of Heaven and Earth, of masculine and feminine balancing, of the story of Jesus and the woman at the well — all harmonising and flowing united back to the Source.

AFFIRMATION: I am at one with my creative source.

Characteristic:	Resourcefulness
Colour:	Aquamarine
Gem Stone:	Aquamarine
Bird:	Wild Geese
Element:	Water
Planet:	Moon and Neptune
System:	Reproductive
Ogham:	UPRIGHT: By constantly cleansing old emotions, you are living out the destiny and bringing to the Earth your own hidden resources.
	REVERSED: You could be travelling in the wrong direction or ignoring the roots from which you came.

conróis / wild rose

Common Names: Wild Rose, Briar Rose, Wild Briar

ROSACEAE *Canina*

DESCRIPTION: Wild Rose is a bushy shrub which can produce woody stems. Leaves are oval with toothed margins and may be pale red especially when newly opened. Flowers are single, white or pink with five petals and a lovely fragrance. The fruit is the familiar rose-hip: a bright red, pulpy seed vessel. They are found most often in hedgerows. Height to 6 feet (2 m).

Angels have been a source of comfort to men and women since the Earth was created. How much closer to an Angel can we get in Nature than through the scent of the Rose?

Scents and perfumes in nature open up the senses to the awakening of the New Dawn. As we move in the flow of the Triple Spiral through the weaving and searching, death and rebirth, we come to mastery of ourselves. Like the Rose, we become a source of beauty.

This oil/essence can be used with love, faith and hope for the New Day, for commitment to the Resurrection, for joy along the Path and for the

sojourn when we need to smell a few roses. Put the oil in the palms of your hands at sunrise as a reminder of the New Day and at sunset as a reminder of the Sunset of our lives.

The oil/essence Wild Rose is made from Rosehips and is fragrance-free except to the higher senses. Wild Rose is a bush of the woods.

AFFIRMATION: I am at one with my creative source.

Characteristic:	Creativity
Colour:	Apricot
Gem Stone:	Diamond
Bird:	Phoenix
Element:	Air
Planet:	Jupiter and Venus
System:	Reproductive
Ogham:	UPRIGHT: Through mastery of ourselves, we come to know joy and, then, we can truly dance the dance of the angels.
	REVERSED: To deny love is self destructive, search within the Rose of your heart for your flowering.

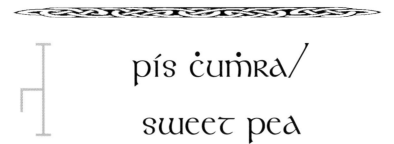

pís ċumra/ sweeτ peá

Common Names: Sweet Pea has many named varieties

Leguminosae *Lathyrus odoratus*

> Description: A climbing plant. Leaves are sharply pointed and come in pairs. The flowers are wonderfully fragrant and come in many colours, mostly whites, pinks and purples. Height from 9 inches (23 cm) to 8 feet (2.5 m).

The Sweet Pea has adorned gardens for many a long day. The idea of sweetness and such variety of colour brings us a sense of the Almighty Sweetness. The notion of the link between the common pea, the sweet pea and pituitary gland (which is the master gland and about the size of a pea), brings alive within us the possibilities of the fires of the Quintessence.

As we create our own garden — our secret, inner garden — we have the freedom to visit and to draw on the sweetness of the Heavenly Garden where everything is offered to us – if only we can receive. Since the Christ note is heard

through the Hormonal System, balance within this system opens the gate to the Heavenly Garden.

This oil/essence is fragrance-free except to the higher senses.

AFFIRMATION: I am balanced between Spirit and matter. I accept the sweetness and abundance of Life and acknowledge my gifts.

Characteristic:	Insight
Colour:	Magenta
Gemstone:	Malachite
Bird:	Chaffinch — Ri Rua
Element:	Fire
Planet:	Venus and Neptune
System:	Glandular
Ogham:	UPRIGHT: You accept graciously the Gifts of the Garden.
	REVERSED: To appreciate the Garden, you need to go through the Garden Gate.

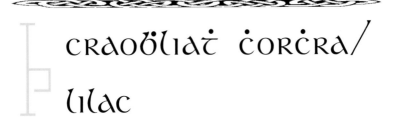

craobliat corcra/ lilac

Common Names: Lilac, Common Lilac with many named single and double varieties

OLEACEAE *Syringa vulgaris*

> DESCRIPTION: Deciduous tree or shrub with suckers. Leaves are ovate or heart-shaped with a strong central rib (up to 6 inches/15 cm long). Flowers are single or double, grow in long, upright panicles and come in many colours ranging from whites to pinks to purples and, of course, lilac. Height to 20 feet (6 m).

The Lilac bush is one of nature's simplest and oldest bushes. The Doctrine of Signatures teaches us that plants have special benefits for us on Earth. The perfume of the lilac delights the senses: a "Heavenly Scent," as it is often called. The lilac is, symbolically, food for thought since it does quite literally feed our brain cells (through the sense of smell or when rubbed into the body or when taken as an essence).

The lilac oil/essence may be used where there has been any disturbance of energy around the brain and crown of the head. The oil may be

rubbed onto the forehead and at the base of the skull. When rubbing in this oil or taking the essence, it is helpful to meditate on the colour lilac and how it graces nature.

This oil/essence is fragrance-free except to the higher senses.

AFFIRMATION: I am balanced between Spirit and matter. I am at one with my environment.

Characteristic:	Inspiration
Colour:	Lilac
Gem Stone:	Gold
Bird:	The Ostrich
Element:	Air
Planet:	Jupiter and Neptune
System:	Glandular
Ogham:	UPRIGHT: The sweetness of life is experienced when the Godhead and self are in unison.
	REVERSED: You have become disconnected to some extent from your Higher self and need to re-establish a better link to the Source.

mαgδαlen

Common Names: Fuschia, Fiúise

ONAGRACEAE *Magellanica*

DESCRIPTION: Deciduous tree or shrub with light brown, peeling bark. Leaves are oval, toothed, short stalked and opposite (1 to 2.5 inches/2.5 to 6 cm long). Flowers are pendulous, crimson-red sepals with a purple centre consisting four petals and eight stamens. Found mostly in hedgerows and gardens. Height to 12 feet (nearly 4 m).

The familiar story of Magdalen waiting in the garden in the dawn for the Risen Christ is always with us. Magdalen's pain is understood by those who are undergoing great pain themselves in the quest for the liberation of their own souls. The same Magdalen who embraces the baby is also the Queen of Destruction, the destroyer of the old and outworn. Birth and death are familiar to Magdalen.

Encompassed within the feminine principle is the possibility of encountering the Resurrected Christ in the dawn of a changing day. Her dark and light sides are found in the Spiral, her mastery is found within the creation of the Earth, her pain in the starving child, her beauty in an octave. Magdalen is among us, waiting for each of us to set her

free.

The oil can be rubbed into the pulses or the essence can be taken as you think about the liberation of the feminine principle and the journey back to the Source of Life.

AFFIRMATION: I am indestructible. Come what may, I am loved.

Characteristic: Liberation
Colour: Pearl
Gem Stone: Rose Quartz
Bird: Oystercatcher
Element: Air
Planet: Moon and Uranus
Balancer

Ogham: UPRIGHT: Because you are a true disciple, your love is fathomless. Courage and perseverance will bring you home.

                   REVERSED: Your enslavement is self-imposed. You need to free the chains in order to see the new day.

ꝼaiꝺla Rua/

coppeR ꝺeech

Common Names: Copper Beech

FAGACEAE *Fagus sylvatica* f. "Purpurea"

> DESCRIPTION: Bark is grey and smooth on a massive trunk. The tree is well shaped with a huge spread providing dense shade. Leaves (4 inches/10 cm) are copper to purple. They are oval shaped and pointed. The edges are wavy at the vein end. The flowers are catkins producing the beech mast containing 2 (usually) glossy, brown, pyramidal shaped nuts which are protected by a bristly exterior which splits into four parts to release them. They are woodland trees and often are planted for ornamental reasons. Height to 130 feet (40 m).

Cooper Beech is distinctive because of its colour. It stands out amid the greenery of the countryside. Copper is the element that connects base metals to semi-precious stones. It is also the best conductor of electricity. It is the spark of life-force.

Since the spirit of life is the key to the kidneys, Copper Beech oil/essence can be a wonderful help when we are linking our lower and higher

selves, when the life force may have become weak as a result of this stress and, therefore, is in need of stimulation.

AFFIRMATION: I accept the sweetness and abundance of Life and acknowledge my gifts. I accept with courage the Divine flow.

Characteristic:	Courage
Colour:	Copper
Gem Stone:	Gold
Bird:	Peacock
Element:	Air
Planet:	Saturn and Uranus
System:	Urinary
Ogham:	UPRIGHT: You have the courage to be different and therefore a messenger for the Creator.
	REVERSED: The joys of life elude you. You need to look at your own infinity.

áirne / sloe

Common Names: Sloe is the fruit of the Blackthorn

ROSACEAE *Prunus spinosa*

DESCRIPTION: Shrub-like with dark, thorny bark often found in hedgerows. In a grove, it may form a canopy and send out sucker roots. Leaf is toothed, dark-green, elliptical and comes to a point at both ends. It has prominent veins and a leathery appearance. Dense clouds of white flowers with gold tipped anthers cover the tree before the leaves appear. The resulting fruits look like plums and are dark purple but are bitter. Height to 16 feet (5 m).

As the Sloe (the fruit of the Blackthorn – lower division of the wood) ripens in Autumn, the tendency for the young inexperienced children is to pick the fruit and eat it. There is sometimes laughter as the child's face winces from the bitterness of the Sloe.

The lessons may be difficult through Blackthorn and Sloe which allow no choices. However, experience teaches that sometimes, to learn, we must taste the bitter fruit. The sharpness of the taste of the Sloe speaks to us about the need for vigilance in what we are "ingesting." Also, having tasted the depths of the bitterness, we may

then appreciate the Almighty sweetness.

This Ogham Oil or essence is good for us when we are experiencing the lesson which is teaching us to sharpen up.

AFFIRMATION: I move forward with ease and grace.

Characteristic:	Acceptance
Colour:	Red
Gem Stone:	Onyx
Bird:	Curlew
Element:	Fire
Planet:	Saturn
System:	Muscular
Ogham:	UPRIGHT: You will come to resurrection through accepting bitter gall.
	REVERSED: As a child of the Universe, you need to accept that you are your own teacher.

giúis/pine

Common Names: Pine, Scots Pine, Scotch Fir, Péine Albanach

PINACEAE *Pinus sylvestris* Linnaeus

DESCRIPTION: Bark on this tree is quite distinctive as, near the ground, it starts out greyish to purplish dark brown with deep, irregular fissures then, in the upper reaches, it becomes quite smooth and flakes off. leaving a characteristic reddish-orange-brown color. Needles are flat, dark green with a blue-grey or blue-green tint, occur in pairs and are

up to 2.75 inches (7 cm) long. Cones start off green and egg-shaped and mature slowly over a three year period – at which time, they are brown and woody and release their seeds. These pines will flourish on mountainsides even in poor, gravely or sandy soil. Height to 115 feet (35 m).

Standing close to the pine (a noble of the wood), we become aware of the tree. The "needles" of the tree might tell us: if we are blaming others, we could find ourselves needling them. If we are blaming ourselves, we could become fissured like the bark of the Pine.

The Ogham oil/essence of the pine is cleansing. As we come to the end of the Piscean Age, this Ogham teaches us to release blame and guilt and to forgive ourselves and others. Just as there are many different varieties of pine, guilt and blame also portray themselves in many different forms. This oil/essence will help dissolve guilt and blame, making way for love to flow.

AFFIRMATION: I release the need for conflict. I radiate peace from the centre of my being. I accept with courage the Divine flow.

Characteristic:	Peace/Compassion/Generosity
Colour:	Green
Gem Stone:	Clear Quartz
Bird:	Cross-bill

Element:	Water
Planet:	Pluto and Moon
System:	Urinary
Ogham:	UPRIGHT: When it is realised that there is no guilt and no blame, the spirit of life blossoms in the power of that moment.
	REVERSED: You could be losing your power through the poisons of guilt and blame.

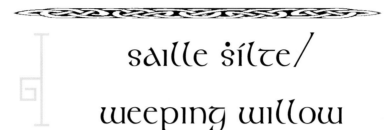

saille silte/

weeping willow

Common Names: Weeping Willow, Chinese Weeping Willow, Golden Weeping Willow

SALICACEAE *Salix babylonica* Linnaeus (Chinese) and SALICACEAE *Salix* x *chrysocoma* (Golden)

> DESCRIPTION: Bark is grey-brown, though the Golden form has golden-yellow branches. The trunk will be fissured. Leaves are much longer (4.75 inches/ 12 cm) than wide (.75 inches/2 cm), toothed, green on top with bluish-grey undersides and become smooth when mature. Flowers are catkins which produce seeds released in a puffy white down. Like all willow, this tree likes damp locations, such as meadowlands and near rivers. Height to 65 feet (20 m).

The Weeping Willow (commoner of the wood) talks of being laden down emotionally. The load that we have to carry may weigh us down, sometimes to the extent of being unbearable. It can be very difficult to stand aside and watch others learn difficult lessons. But what are our choices?

Since the weeping willow is water loving, it teaches us that the tears fall into the Earth again,

to reconnect to the roots and to the waters of life, bringing about an emotional balance.

AFFIRMATION: I am indestructible. Come what may, I am loved.

Characteristic:	Unconditional Love
Colour:	Turquoise
Gem Stone:	Turquoise
Bird:	Cormorant
Element:	Water
Planet:	Moon and Neptune
Balancer	
Ogham:	UPRIGHT: True love is allowing others to learn their lessons even though it is painful for you.
	REVERSED: You are hindering growth. You need to stand aside and allow others their space while they learn.

seiceamar/

sycamore

Common Names: Sycamore, Summer Tree, Great Maple, Mock Plane, Seiceamar, Seiceamóir, Crann Bán

ACERACEAE *Acer pseudoplatanus* Linnaeus

DESCRIPTION: Bark is smooth and grey when young, developing cracks which flake off when older making patches of different colors from pinkish to yellowish-green. Tree is tall and sturdy with a large trunk, dense foliage and many branches in every

direction. In the Spring, the twigs are noticeably stout with large green buds covered in scales which may be green edged with black or downy pink depending on the variety. The leaves are very large (up to 7 inches/18 cm long and often wider than long) with a very long leaf stalk (up to 8 inches/20 cm) and are characterized by five deeply cut, pointed, irregularly toothed lobes. The leaves appear with or slightly after the flowers which hang in long panicles of up to 100 yellow-green flowers. The fruits are winged seeds found in pairs (or rarely three or six) joined at a 90° angle. Sycamores prefer dry soil in woodlands on mountainsides. Height to 115 feet (35 m).

As we watch the "wings" of the sycamore fly from the tree in Autumn, we are reminded of the perfection of the aerodynamics of nature. The wings spin as they fly, talking to us of a safe landing and a new rooting. Since the spin is free flowing, there is no resistance or conflict and the destination is reached safely. This flight is reflective of the Triple Spiral.

As a prolific propagator, the Sycamore abundantly spreads its seeds of freedom everywhere with great self-assurance. With enough confidence, we can let go of mental control, allowing Higher energies to work. Hence, the oil/essence of this Ogham promotes a freer flow in the digestive system.

AFFIRMATION: I let go of old patterns and absorb Life's lessons with wisdom and joy. I accept the sweetness and abundance of Life and acknowledge my gifts.

Characteristic:	Confidence
Colour:	Orange
Gem Stone:	Moss Agate
Bird:	Swift
Element:	Earth
Planet:	Sun, Venus and Uranus
System:	Digestive
Ogham:	UPRIGHT: You are free flowing and absorb change easily.
	REVERSED: By not absorbing, you are prolonging your journey. You need to trust the spirit of the wind.

cnó capaill/

horse chestnut

Common Names: Horse Chestnut, Common Horse Chestnut, Giant's Nosegay, Crann Cnó Capaill

HIPPOCASTANACEAE *Aesculus hippocastanum* Linnaeus

DESCRIPTION: Bark is grey-brown to red-brown which flakes away in large scales. Trunk is massive and usually undivided. The twigs, having characteristic horseshoe shaped leaf scars, are quite fat with huge, dark (blackish, brownish or even purplish), sticky, scaly buds which are the largest of any tree in this country. The leaves break out of the bud scales in fan folds becoming pear shaped, finely toothed, pointed and very long (up to 10 inches/ 25 cm). They occur in opposite pairs without stalks in a compound of 5 to 7 leaflets of unequal size. Flowers are a quite lovely white with pinkish-crimson splotches growing in an upright cluster and looking like large candles from a distance. The fruits mature in spiny shells which split to reveal 1 to 3 shiny, round, hard, inedible nuts or conkers. Horse chestnuts prefer woodlands, especially on mountainsides, and are often found in hedgerows. Height to 115 feet (35 m).

The Horse Chestnut is one of the favourite trees of young and old. Today, children continue to play the traditional game of conkers. Children's games, nursery rhymes, fairy tales and, indeed, our total mythologies teach us so much. So, too, can the game of conkers teach us 'older' children about breaking down our own shell and finding our own nourishment.

As our shell or skeleton needs repair and we need revitalising, we could look to this Ogham Oil/Essence. We are the fruit – the product – of our ancestry. Through a process of self-discovery, we can develop the hidden strands of our inherited DNA in a natural way. Like conkers ripened by

the golden sun, Gold aids the physical structure and cell regeneration.

Since the skeleton of the physical body tells its own story, so also does the grouse tell its story by making human sounds which say, "Go back." These sounds give us the clue to look back at our own ancestry for the key to our present condition. Once known, we can heal not only the past but, also, the present and the future.

Affirmation: I am supported in Life.

Characteristic:	Self-discovery
Colour:	Gold
Gem Stone:	Snow Quartz
Bird:	Grouse
Element:	Earth
Planet:	Sun, Saturn and Pluto
System:	Skeleton
Ogham:	Upright: The versatility of the Horse Chestnut allows you the freedom to work beneath the surface to find your nourishment.
	Reversed: Your shell has become impenetrable. Go back to the game of conkers to find the golden fruit.

spirizual rescue

Common Names: Magnolia. Many named varieties.

MAGNOLIACEAE *x Soulangeana*

DESCRIPTION: Smooth grey bark on a deciduous tree or shrub. The dark green, glossy and smooth leaves are a long ellipse (up to 8 inches/20 cm) about 4.75 inches/12 cm wide ending in a short point. Flowers are white shaded with purplish-pink or violet with an upright habit and shaped like a goblet until opened wide as a saucer. The fruits are borne in an erect cylindrical cluster (4 inches/10 cm). Magnolias are found in the garden. Height to 30 feet (9 m).

The Magnolia Tree is beautiful in early Summer. The white flowers are a joy to look at as they open up to the warm sun. Where the branch meets the flower, the stem is violet and the colour is also visible on the underside and inside the base of the flower. This infusion of the violet colour teaches us about the infusion of spiritual energies into the body of the flower.

Sometimes when we are in a very negative state, we can lose sight of these spiritual energies and the source from which they come. The white flowers allow us to focus on the delicacy of the subtle

energies of the body and soul as they become frayed from our struggle.

This oil/essence helps where there has been a debilitating spiritual struggle, severe shock, accidents, serious illness. It is especially useful for healing and soothing in hospitals, hospices and with the terminally ill.

AFFIRMATION: I am indestructible. Come what may, I am loved.

Characteristic:	Transmutation
Colour:	Apricot
Gem Stone:	Clear Quartz
Bird:	Dove
Element:	Ether
Planet:	Neptune and Saturn
Balancer	
Ogham:	UPRIGHT: You accept the link between the womb and the tomb.
	REVERSED: You are avoiding reality. You need to look on this phase as a new birth.

Reaóóig/bog myrtle

Common Names: Bog Myrtle, Common Myrtle, Roideóg, Sweet Gale

Myricaceae *Myrica gale* L.

DESCRIPTION: A deciduous bush or shrub with fragrant shoots. The dark green, slightly glossy leaves are spear-shaped and 2.5 inches/6 cm long to nearly 1 inch/2 cm wide. Flowers are catkins. Favorite habitats are the boglands, wet moorlands and lakeshores. Height to 6 feet (2 m).

Traditionally, Myrtle was placed in the wedding bouquets. It is also related that lovers used to stand in Myrtle groves and pledge their troth.

Bog Myrtle (a bush of the wood) likes plenty of space in which to grow and usually chooses the bog. Myrtle offers us an opportunity to create more space within our bodies. As we breathe deeply, we create this space in the areas where air meets fire.

By planting more myrtle, we can create space in the environment. Thereby, we also create space (air) for the "trees of the body" (lungs). In turn, this exchange of gasses may take place more efficiently due to the special qualities of Bog Myrtle.

By acknowledging Spirit on the breath, our connections are deepened into the Earth where our roots are in the past and our branches in the present.

AFFIRMATION: I claim and am safe within my own space. I am immune to destructive influences.

Characteristic:	Space
Colour:	Electric Blue
Gem Stone:	Amazonite
Bird:	Sparrow
Element:	Air
Planet:	Venus and Uranus
System:	Auric – Subtle Bodies
Ogham:	UPRIGHT: Since you have created such space for yourself, your possibilities for expression are endless.
	REVERSED: Since fire needs oxygen to fuel it, you need to clear the clutter from the passageways.

leamán/elm

Common Names: Wych Elm, Leamhán Sléibhe

ULMACEAE *Ulmus glabra*

DESCRIPTION: Bark starts out grey and smooth on young trees, becoming scaly and fissured with age. The large leaves (up to 7 inches/18 cm) come to a tapering point and are very unequal at the stalk end. In fact, one side of the leaf will grow so high on its stalk as to quite cover it. They are hairy on both sides with the top side being very rough and have very prominent veins. The tiny red flowers, which appear before the leaves, grow in clusters on one-year old twigs. The fruit is papery, oval shaped with a seed held in the centre and appears

before the leaves are out. Elm likes hedgerows and woodlands. Height to 130 feet (40 m) and is often wider than it is tall.

In old Irish manuscripts, there are stories about the sacredness of the Elm. One such tree grew at Clonmacnoise on the River Shannon: one evening, a leper named Comlech placed some holy relics in a hole in the trunk of the tree. Next morning, the tree had healed and the relics had been swallowed. When he tried to cut the tree open to retrieve them, the wood chips stuck to the tree again. My understanding of this story is that the Elm is receptive and this story tells us that it does indeed absorb.

The reproduction of the layers without discarding or cleansing the previous layers is part of the history of the Elm. For 10,000 years, the Elm has waited to help free humanity from the cycle of the malfunctioning unfriendly cell. The master cells of the body hold the key to the inner world. Finding the right key at the right time opens yet another door to our blueprint.

Elm oil/essence has within it the possibility of raising the vibrations in order to make the door accessible. The fine tuning of the breath in harmony with leamhán offers a passage to the door accelerating a different form of renewal, regeneration and release.

The Elm (a commoner of the wood) is a perfectly balanced tree (yin and yang) and holds the imprint of the memory of the blueprint, thus it helps to free up karma. Elm links us to our source through remembrance.

AFFIRMATION: I release the need for conflict. I radiate peace from the centre of my being.

Characteristic:	Release
Colour:	Cyan
Gem Stone:	Gold
Bird:	Crow
Element:	Fire
Planet:	Saturn, Uranus and Pluto
System:	Auric – Subtle Bodies
Ogham:	UPRIGHT: By remembering who you really are, you can clear a passageway to the door of release.
	REVERSED: The conflict you are caught in consciously or unconsciously is keeping the door closed to your Divine Face. Clear your memory.

cantabillae

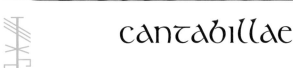

In the absence of self-love, there exists conflict with the self and avoidance of our true Reality. The Angel Cantabillae (under the protection of Raphael) holds the key to the door of self-love. At this door, we are invited to grace ourselves for the dance of the Angel Cantabillae. Dancing and moving with the wind through our hair, feeling the Earth under our feet, feeding our senses on the aromas of herbs, flowers, plants and trees, watching and feeling the pulse of the planet, tasting the mists of mystery is to grace the sacred Ogham and the Angel Cantabillae. Dancing in a Rainbow, brings many colours to our coat and offers us the possibility of becoming a Rainbow ourselves.

As the thymus opens enough for us to hug ourselves, we strengthen our Aqua-aura vibration and become the dancer and the dance. Within this dance, there is only love since everything else is an illusion.

AFFIRMATION: I am indestructible. Come what may, I am loved.

Characteristic:	Self-love
Colour:	Aqua

Gem Stone:	Aqua-aura (quartz in fused with gold)
Bird:	Kestrel
Element:	Ether
Planet:	Venus and Neptune
System:	Auric – Subtle Bodies
Ogham:	UPRIGHT: Self-love is the dance of the angels. You are a shining light in the new dawn.
	REVERSED: Your lack of self-love is affecting your thymus gland. The door is always open with a fire in the hearth.

meeshla

DESCRIPTION: A mixture of Pine (described above) and Cedar of Lebanon (PINACEAE *Cedrus libani* A. Richard). The bark of the Cedar is greenish to greyish brown that crack and fissure into plates. The trunk is enormous and the branches characteristically flatten out vertically. The flattened top makes this tree easy to distinguish from other cedars. The dark green to blue/grey green needles (1.25 inches/3 cm) are hard and clump up in swirls of 10 to 20 tufts. The Cedar has obvious male (2 inches/5 cm) and female (5.5 inches/14 cm) upright, barrel-shaped flowers resulting in the purplish brown cones which take three years to mature. They thrive in the forests on mountainsides and are widely planted as ornamentals. Height to 130 feet (40 m).

To rediscover the subtleness of the Fairy Princess in ourselves is to rediscover part of our own Divine magic. Meeshla, the Princess energy of the ancient ones of our land, offers the dying King a soothing, peaceful cup. Her gentleness and strength help cast a mantle of peace and harmony over us and our land. Born out of conflict, this oil/essence soothes and feeds the soul with the peace of the Pine and the strength of the Cedar.

If we are disconnected with the antiquity of ourselves, we lose our tie to the subtleness in the

very core of ourselves. Meeshla helps us to make the re-connection to that subtleness with ourselves and with the Earth. Meeshla is the power of gentleness.

AFFIRMATION: I release the need for conflict. I radiate peace from the centre of my being.

Characteristic:	Peace
Colour:	Apple Green
Gem Stone:	Olivine (Pele's Tears*)
Bird:	Stonechat
Element:	Earth
Planet:	Sun and Pluto
System:	Auric – Subtle Bodies
Ogham:	UPRIGHT: With the initiation of Cedar comes peace and harmony.
	REVERSED: You need to release the need for conflict.

*Pele is the Hawaiian Goddess of fire and volcanoes. Pele is pronounced Peh'leh.

Autumn Beeches

TO A TREE

My Dear Tree, what has become of thee?
Until lately, you have been clad so beautifully.
You look gaunt, naked and stark
As you face your winter in the dark.

My Dear Tree, you have cast your beautiful
possessions,
All cared for without obsessions.
You have scattered Autumn's Clothing
And face, with grace, Winter's not knowing.

My Dear Tree, deep rooted in the Earth,
You have descended to your depths.
In moonlight's shadows, you wait:
Searching, seeking, pruning.

My Dear Tree, I look at you and feel your pain.
Unmasked, you embrace all searching gales,
Buffeted and torn by wind and hail,
Share no sunshine yet or comforting rays.

My Dear Tree, how many spirals in your trunk?
You have truth to tell of death and birth
And ever repeating pattern trends.
Oh, that I could have your blend.

My Dear Tree, you are poetry.
I watch you move but not your roots.
And, as cold winds cease to blow,
You will bring me hope out of winter's snow.

HAND OGHAM

Hand Ogham is an ancient form of healing. The hands in themselves tell their own story. The hands mirror each other and the whole person. Each finger carries its own ability to link into deep levels of healing. Since we have two hands, we are talking about Right and Left, Conscious and Subconscious, Masculine and Feminine. Balance in life is integrating all aspects of duality.

Through the hands, we establish a tangible link with our Universe. With the hands, we give and take, traditionally giving with the Right and receiving with the Left. We shake hands as a form of greeting and as a way of sealing an agreement. Through our hands, we can make our imagination a Reality through our Creativity. We use the hands to help express what we wish to say and to give emphasis to our language. We hold hands as a sign of friendship. We use our hands to comfort, caress and heal ourselves and others. In folk dances, we hold hands as we dance the circle. The fingers carry the genetic blueprint of our identity and the eternal blueprint of the Spiral.

In our language, we refer to the hands to help us express our situation. Consider these expressions: empty handed, hands full, a handful, needing a hand, many hands, great hands, hands on

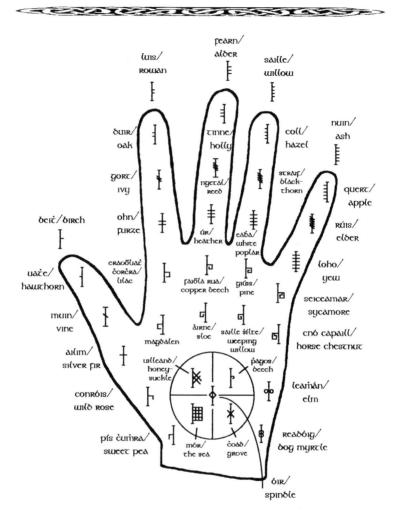

deck, handy, nimble fingers, all thumbs. As we hold our hands together in prayer, we are creating wholeness within ourselves and bringing into balance all aspects of our person.

Deaf people use sign language. In ancient times, the Druids communicated in Ogham by touching the points on the hand associated with the different letters/Oghams. Complex ideas could be conveyed as well as simply spelling out the words. They did also use the nose or shin and the five fingers to make the Ogham signs. This secret language was later made illegal because of the power it gave the initiates.

Since the fingers and hands represent the whole person, the systems of the body may be helped to harmonise through Hand Ogham. The Ogham is a language of signs and symbols, representing the language, philosophy and healing of each tree. Symbols of themselves are beyond language and, like Oils and Essences, work on the subconscious. Hand Ogham involves the application of Ogham Oils on specific points on the hands which access the entire body. Using oils on the hands is a way of connecting and linking into the "Tree of Life."

CELTIC TREE OF LIFE

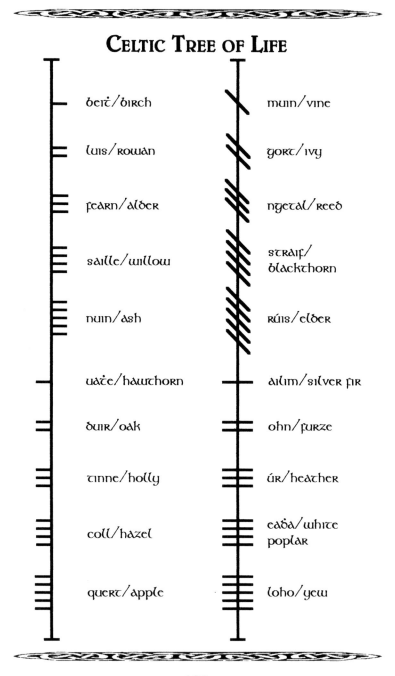

beiṫ/birch

luis/rowan

fearn/alder

saille/willow

nuin/ash

uaṫe/hawthorn

duir/oak

tinne/holly

coll/hazel

quert/apple

muin/vine

gort/ivy

ngetal/reed

straif/
blackthorn

rúis/elder

ailim/silver fir

ohn/furze

úr/heather

eada/white
poplar

loho/yew

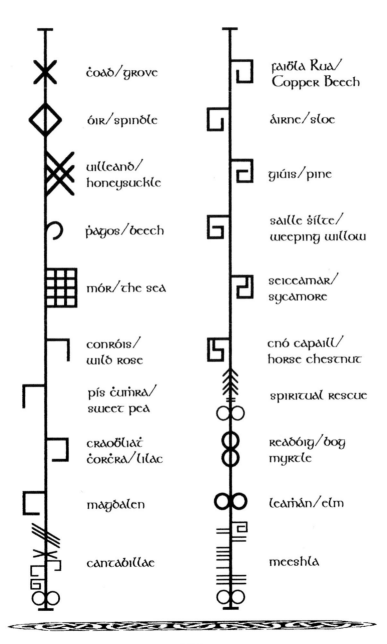

coað/grove

óir/spindle

uilleand/
honeysuckle

paġos/beech

mór/the sea

conróis/
wild rose

pís cumra/
sweet pea

craoibiac
corcra/lilac

magdalen

cantabillae

faiðla Rua/
Copper Beech

áirne/sloe

giúis/pine

saille śílte/
weeping willow

seiceamar/
sycamore

cnó capaill/
horse chestnut

spiritual rescue

readóig/bog
myrtle

leamán/elm

meeshla

REFLEXOLOGY

Reflexology is an ancient science and art which deals with the theory that all organs of the body have nerve endings in the hands and feet. The hands and feet have reflexes relating the totality of the person: body, mind and spirit. When we become ill or out of tune with ourselves, toxins build up at the nerve endings. By massaging these points on the feet, the toxins are broken down and the body can heal itself.

As we heal and change, we can feel subtle changes in our feet. If we put our "foot in it," we have made a mistake. As we put our right foot forward, we are making our best effort.

To do justice to the benefits of Reflexology is a book in itself. Suffice it to say that the feet are our connection with the Earth. The Earth generously gives to us through the feet and we feel the pulse or energy of Mother Earth. If we are well "Earthed," we are able to "ground" wisdom and bring it into the market place, thereby spiritualising our efforts and making the best possible use of resources.

The Master Jesus showed us that the washing and anointing of the feet was an important part of the lives of the ancients. Jesus' own feet were washed and treated with oils by Mary Magdalen.

It would seem that massaging the feet was part of everyday life in some cultures throughout the ages.

Ogham oils can be used successfully for massaging and anointing the feet. See the next section for how to choose and use the oils for maximum benefit. Healthy feet keep us rooted and firmly planted just like the roots of the tree keep the tree firmly rooted and planted.

How well planted are you?

HOW TO USE THE OILS*

First of all, choose whichever three trees and oils speak to you. This choice may be based on your needs now, linked to your intuition and/or chosen according to the systems that require healing. The oils come bottled one tree oil per bottle or as systemic oils containing three or more oils. Rub the oils into the hands or feet at the relevant points until you feel that you have integrated them. The oil can be rubbed into the hands as described in the Hand Ogham chart (page 178) — each point is linked to the Ogham symbol and the tree. When rubbing in the oil, it is beneficial to look at the symbol associated with it and to meditate on the particular philosophy of the tree. In this way, we are acting out of a Trinity of seeing, being and doing.

The oils may be used:

     ⊲   in the bath. Any number of drops up to 12 may be added to the water.

     ⊲   may be added to other oils for burning. The vibration of other oils is increased and the aromatic effect is

* These Oils and Essences may support healing of disturbances of energy of the systems of the body. If symptoms persist, consult a medical practitioner.

greater. The aroma of burning Ogham oils is very subtle and effects the senses in a healing way.

 for anointing the senses as a blessing.

 for burning in churches, temples and other places of worship.

 for cleansing heavy vibrations and atmospheres. Best effects are achieved by burning the oils on their own or with other oils.

 for Reflexology of the feet, hands and ears. A few drops of warmed Ogham oil of the person's choice are very healing and soothing.

 along with Aromatherapy oils, the effects of which can be deep and lasting.

 in hospices and hospitals.

 to help recreate the balance of energy needed for harmony.

How To Use The Essences*

Again, choose whichever three trees speak to
you. The essences also come bottled one tree
essence per bottle or as systemic essences containing three or more essences. While the essences may taken internally, they may be used
in the same ways as the oils above. Generally
speaking, however, the oils are for external use
and the essences are for internal use.

The essences may additionally be used:

    ⊲   by adding 5 to 15 drops to your
           drinking water or other beverage.

    ⊲   the same dosage can be put directly
           on the tongue as needed.

    ⊲   added to soups or other dishes af-
           ter cooking.

* These Oils and Essences may support healing of disturbances
of energy of the systems of the body. If symptoms persist, consult a medical practitioner.

Triple Spiral from centre chamber,
Brú na Bóinne (Newgrange)

How To Use The Cards:
Triple Spiral Consultation With
Celtic Tree Ogham Symbols

1.   Decide on a focus for your session with the cards (for example, your health or job or a certain situation) or simply ask a general question like, "What do I need to know right now?" Write this question or focus down. You can also hold it silently within. Shuffle the cards in any manner. Cut them if you wish.

2.   Pick 5 Ogham Cards and lay them out as follows:

    (a) North; (b) South; (c) East; (d) West; (e) Ether

North (a)

West (d)   Ether (e)   East (c)

South (b)

3.   You may photocopy the page with the consultation layout on it on which you can record the cards chosen. Or write out your

answer out on a separate sheet of paper:

(a) North = Sunbeam
(b) South = Root
(c) East = Sap
(d) West = Fruit
(e) Centre = Ether

This choice of symbols represents the past.

4. Next, replace these five cards and now choose five more and repeat the above process. These Oghams represent the present.

5. Replace these cards and now choose another five Symbols. These Oghams represent the future.

6. Now start with the choice of the first selection representing the past and read each card that you received. For additional understanding, consider these additional questions to help you deepen your comprehension of each card. The Ogham Symbols, if drawn reversed, would indicate a negative philosophy of the tree.

Start with the North/Sunbeam.
        What has the sun been shining on?
        Was the sun getting to the trees?

Are there other branches of other trees blocking the sun?

What was the sun's strength for the trees?

What pattern has the sunbeam been making?

Did the tree like the heat of the sun?

How was the wind blowing on the trees?

Did the tree find the breeze cooling or uncomfortable?

Did the tree need more sun than it was getting?

Was the sun able to penetrate the outer layers?

Is the light blinding?

Have you been able to look at the Sun-beam?

Now look at: the South/Root.

How have the roots been?

What sort of soil have they been growing up in?

Have they choked?

Has the air been getting to them?

How deeply embedded have they been?

Have the roots been allowed to grow as deep in the Earth as was necessary?

If the answer is no, why not?

If the root system isn't any good, did the wind blow it over?

Have the roots been nourished?
Has the dead wood been moved from
   about them?
Have there been parasites attacking the
   roots?
Have they been compatible with other
   root systems?

The East/Sap:
   Has the sap been nourished?
   Has it risen in the tree?
   Has it been bled away?
   Has it dried up?
   What would have started its flow again?
   Has the sap been healthy?
   Was it attracted upwards toward the sun
      or was it happy to stay near the root?

The West/Fruit:
   Did the tree produce fruit?
   What was the quality of the fruit?
   Was it a good crop?
   Could the crop have been improved?
   Was the fruit ready before its time or not
      ready in time?
   Was it artificially ripened or ripened natu-
      rally by the sun from within itself?
   Was the climate suitable?
   Was the fruit for sharing?
   Was it sweet or sour?

Centre/Ether:

> How has spirit affected all these processes?
>
> Has it been allowed to affect them like it should?
>
> How have the processes all reacted to the central energy that has surrounded them?
>
> If the tree has not been growing properly, which of the processes would have needed looking at to allow balance to prevail in the growth of the tree?
>
> What destructive forces have been pulling against healthy growth?
>
> Was the tree pruned?
>
> If so, how was it affected?
>
> Which direction do we need to work in to see where these destructive forces have been? North, South, East, West?

6. Now, repeat this entire process with the second set of symbols (present) and the third set (future).

If some Symbols come up more than once, there is particular emphasis on this Ogham and you will need to note where they are. Oils or essences could be given as a treatment on the basis of any recurring Symbols.

NOTES:

LAYOUT FOR TRIPLE SPIRAL CONSULTATION

Past:
(a) North — Sunbeam
(b) South — Root
(c) East — Sap
(d) West — Fruit
(e) Centre — Ether

(a)

(d) (e) (c)

(b)

Present:
(a) North — Sunbeam
(b) South — Root
(c) East — Sap
(d) West — Fruit
(e) Centre — Ether

(a)

(d) (e) (c)

(b)

Future:
(a) North — Sunbeam
(b) South — Root
(c) East — Sap
(d) West — Fruit
(e) Centre — Ether

(a)

(d) (e) (c)

(b)

NOTES:

MINI-CONSULTATION

As desired, three Symbols could be chosen at any time to focus on some particular matter: one to represent the past, one the present and one the future.

The question which is presented can be written on a sheet of paper or simply held in the person's head. You will probably want to date and record your answers.

The apple does not fall

far from the tree.

The Unravelling

One day, when I was searching for some answers about what was deep inside myself, I remember looking at a tree and asking the tree a question. One question led to another. Before I knew it, I had a list of questions that I was asking the tree. I found that the tree did give me answers and it challenged me in some way to get to the root and branches of myself. The tree said, "My roots are in the past. My branches are in the present."

I discovered that the tree helped me to unravel myself and revealed to me the story of my own journey. Asking those questions led me into the whole area of my own ancestry and a realization that I carried, in the DNA, memories and traits from the past. I suggested this method to some family members who came up with more questions. The questions below are the results of this brainstorming. See if you can come up with your own questions. (Space is provided at the end for your own notes.)

I invite you to freely use these questions as a workbook to establish your own communication with trees and, therefore, a deeper communication with yourself and with others. One method would be to sit by the tree, get comfortable, close your eyes and meditate with the tree. After a

while, you may feel the tree beginning to reveal its secrets. Another method would be to use the questions in a group workshop. Also, if you can't get outside or near one of the trees in this book that you'd like to get to know, you can meditate with a picture of it or with the oil or essence of the tree itself. Follow your own instincts in relation to what you need to do.

Dear Tree:

1. Who are you?
2. Why are you growing here?
3. How long have you been here?
4. How long is your life?
5. Where did you come from?
6. Why are you that shape? Why are your leaves that shape?
7. How did you remember to grow the way you are?
8. How deep are your roots?
9. How big will you grow?
10. Where are your parents?
11. Who do you most resemble – Father or Mother?
12. Did you know your granny? Who is Brigid?
13. Did you ever hear talk of your grandfather?
14. Do you have offspring?
15. Where are they?
16. How do you spread your seeds?
17. Where do you spread them?
18. Did they tell you about your family tree?

19. How has your nearest human family treated you?
20. Has any family asked you to be their family tree?
21. What would you do with a black sheep?
22. Who was your last close relative that died?
23. What were the circumstances?
24. Did you grieve properly?
25. Are you afraid of dying?
26. Have you ever helped people heal memories of the past?
27. In your personal relationships, are your ties life giving or destructive?
28. Who are your friends?
29. Did Heather, Violet or Rosemary call to see you lately?
30. How do you feel about other trees?
31. How do they feel about you?
32. Do you attract others who are like you?
33. Do you attract people who need you?
34. Do you have a link with your species in other places?
35. Do you have good neighbours?
36. What is it like in your space?
37. What animals do you shade?
38. What birds nest in you?
39. Where is your favourite place?
40. Do you like tree houses?
41. What flowers grow beside you?
42. Do you enjoy the company of children?
43. When you were young were you ever hurt?

44.   Were you ever blamed for anything?
45.   Do you feel sheltered or exposed?
46.   Do you feel nurtured or neglected?
47.   Do you feel protected or polluted?
48.   Have you ever been honoured?
49.   Have you ever been abused?
50.   What is your medicine ?
51.   Do you ever suffer from disease? How does illness affect you?
52.   Who uses you and why?
53.   Does the jigsaw puzzle you?
54.   Does the jig puzzle saw you?
55.   How do you feel about pruning?
56.   How do you experience the human cycle?
57.   How many generations of people have you seen come and go?
58.   How do you feel about your relationship with humans?
59.   At the last picnic near you, what were they talking about?
60.   What do you breathe in and breathe out?
61.   Who or what are you most dependent on?
62.   Have you many friends?
63.   Do you have sympathy or empathy for others?
64.   Are you yielding or stiff?
65.   Do you feel privileged in life?
66.   Have you or your ancestors ever been described as sacred?
67.   When the wind speaks through you what is the message?

68. What is your wisdom?
69. What are your gifts?
70. What are you best at?
71. If you were bestowing a precious gift, who would you give it to?
72. When you die, what gifts will you leave behind and what will you take with you?
73. Where will you go?
74. Have you celebrated new birth recently?
75. How did you celebrate?
76. Which is your favourite season?
77. Are you happy with your life?
78. Did you ever laugh?
79. Did you ever cry?
80. Do you ever feel alone?
81. Do you ever get angry?
82. What do you do with your anger?
83. What are your fears?
84. Do you mind being hugged?
85. Were you ever the lone bush?
86. Why do you grow in graveyards?
87. Why do you grow near holy wells?
88. Would it be okay if we danced?
89. Did you ever mark the path of the pilgrimage?
90. Do you wake with the sun?
91. Do you dance in the moonlight?
92. Have you seen God lately?
93. Were you at Calvary?
94. Were you ever the Jesse tree?
95. Could you explain the Tree of Life?

96.   Do you ever wish you had legs?

97.   If you had legs, where would you go?

98.   Does time bother you?

99.   Are you ever hurried or do you live in the moment?

100. Does the formation of your inner circle each year cause you pain?

101. How much change have you lived through?

102. What do you think about lightening?

103. What is your relationship with water, with air, with the Earth and with fire?

104. Do you find it difficult to cope with them?

105. Do you have a relationship with Earth spirits?

106. Who is Pan?

107. Have you heard him?

108. Did you see any fairies lately? How do they dance?

109. What does an Angel look like?

110. Do you have an anam chara (soul friend)?

111. What colour are you today?

112. If you were going to choose a colour to cheer you up today, which colour would you choose?

113. Which is your favourite star?

114. Do you ever dream?

115. Can you imagine the future?

116. What are you hoping for?

117. Are you cosmic?

118. What is your note in the song of life?

119. Are you good at fine-tuning?

120. What is your pitch in the Universal Christ-Note or Ogham?

We ask these questions because we have been wondering and trying to unravel them.

Thank you for your life,

From Your friends at

The Ogham Apothecary
Carlingford
Co. Louth
Ireland
Telephone: +353 (0)42–73793
FAX: +353 (0)42–73839

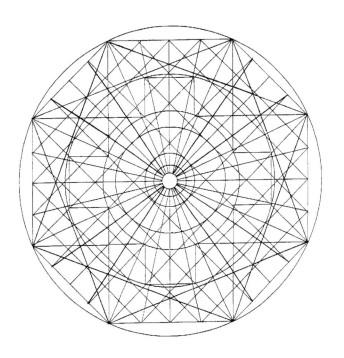

Mandala

This mandala came to me as an expression of the work I had been doing on this book at a particular point in time. It represented to me the totality of the Ogham. Somehow, I could find hidden within it the symbology of the Ogham.

See what you can find in it yourself: a Celtic cross? trees and their Ogham symbols? triangles? circles? stars? the Sun? the Moon? squares? or something else?

As another discovery process, you can use crayons or coloured pens or pencils to create one or more personalized mandalas that would be unique to yourself. It can be very healing to find different patterns in it through colouring. These designs can be imagined as representative of patterns in yourself.

This mandala can also be used as part of a group workshop to deepen your connection with the Universe. See what fun you can have comparing the different designs and shapes among the group.

A SONG OF LIFE

In Spring, I dug in the garden of my soul
The uncultivated, untrodden Earth.
I planted the seeds of growth
And watched them unfold to the sky.

In Summer, I saw them turn golden,
Bathed by fusion of Earth and Light.
I watched butterflies unexpectedly visit
And dark strangers in the night.

In Autumn, I struggled to reap the crop,
Winnowing the chaff from the grain
And, in the golden red sunset,
It seemed like it might be all in vain.

In dark winter, the seeds faced death,
Meditation, investigation, confrontation,
Annihilation, desolation,

And, in unsuspecting moments, revelations of
transformation.

And, as the new dawn of Spring reappears,
Awakening from imprisonment the seeds of
love
To be replanted in the cultured Earth,
They lovingly long for the Light from above.

As tears of healing engulf me like rain,
I feel the freshness in my veins.
On opening my tired eyes I see
That I am becoming what I already am — me.

Relentless, I toil in the garden of love,
Starlight, moonlight, sunlight, insight,
And, as I look in the mirror, I see
That I <u>can</u> become what I already am — me.

Yon lonely thorn, would he could tell
The changes of his parent dell.
. . . .
Would he could tell how deep the shade,
A thousand mingled branches made;
How broad the shadows of the oak,
How clung the rowan to the rock,
And through the foliage showed his head,
With narrow leaves, and berries red;
What pines on every mountain sprung,
O'er every dell what birches hung,
In every breeze what aspens shook,
What alders shaded every brook?

— Sir Walter Scott

BIBLIOGRAPHY

Berger, Terry (ed.). *Garden Proverbs*. London, England: Running Press, 1994

Chase, Pamela Louise & Jonathan Pawlik. *Trees for healing*. North Hollywood, California: Newcastle Publishing Co., Inc., 1991

Coombes, Allen J. *Eyewitness Handbooks: Trees*. *London*, England: Dorling Kindersley, 1992

Culpeper, Nicholas. *Culpeper's Complete Herbal: Consisting of a Comprehensive Description of Nearly All Herbs with Their Medicinal Properties and Directions for Compounding the Medicines Extracted From Them*. London, England: W. Foulsham & Co., Ltd.

Davis, Courtney. *The Celtic Art Source Book*. London, England: Blandford Press, 1988

Davis, Roy Eugene. *An Easy Guide To Meditation*. Lakemont, Georgia: CSA Press, Publishers, 1995

Edlin, Herbert (Text) & Ian Garrard (Illustrations). *The Tree Key: A guide to identification in garden, field and forest*. London, England: Frederick Warne (Publishers) Ltd, 1978

Elwood, Don. *Spiritual Gardening at Its Best.* Blacksburg, Virginia: DiannaQuest Foundation, 1993

Fitter, Alastair (Text) & David More (Illustrations). *Trees.* Glasgow, Scotland: HarperCollins Publishers, 1980

Gorer, Richard. *Illustrated Guide to Trees.* London, England: Kingfisher Books, Ltd., 1980

Greenaway, Theresa. *Pockets: Trees.* London, England: Dorling Kindersley, 1995

Hackney, Paul, editor. *Stewart and Corey's Flora of the North East of Ireland, Third Edition.* Belfast, Northern Ireland: Institute of Irish Studies, The Queen's University of Belfast, 1992.

Hay, Roy and Patrick M. Synge. *The Colour Dictionary of Garden Plants With House and Greenhouse Plants: Published in Collaboration With the Royal Horticulture Society.* London, England: Bloomsbury (Penguin) Books, 1975

Hope, Murry. *Practical Celtic Magic: A Working Guide to the Magical Heritage of the Celtic Races.* Wellingborough, England: The Aquarian Press, 1987

Kelman, Janet Harvey and C. E. Smith. *Trees.* London, England: Thomas Nelson & Sons, Ltd.

Kilbracken, John. *Larousse Easy Way Guide Trees.* London, England: Larousse, 1995

Meyer, Michael R. *A Handbook for the Humanistic Astrologer.* Garden City, New York: Anchor Press/Doubleday, 1974.

Murray, Liz and Colin. *The Celtic Tree Oracle: a System of Divination.* London, England: Rider, 1988

Nelson, E. Charles & Wendy Walsh. *Trees of Ireland.* Dublin, Ireland: The Lilliput Press Ltd, 1993

Paterson, Helena. *The Handbook of Celtic Astrology: The 13-Sign Lunar Zodiac of the Ancient Druids.* St. Paul, MN: Llewellyn Publications, 1994

Rolleston, T.W. *Celtic: Myths and Legends.* London, England: Senate, 1996

Titchiner, Rose, Sue Monk, Rosemary Potter & Patricia Staines. *New Vibrational Flower Essences of Britain and Ireland.* Halesworth, England: Waterlily Books, 1997

Warner, Dick. *Trees: Photoguide.* Glasgow, Scotland: HarperCollins Publishers, 1995

Wilkinson, John (Painter) & Alan Mitchell (Text). *Collins Handguide to the Trees of Britain and Northern Europe.* London, England: William Collins Sons & Co Ltd, 1980.

Wood-Martin, W. G. *Traces of the Elder Faiths of Ireland: A Folklore Sketch: A Handbook of Irish Pre-Christian Traditions, Volume II.* Port Washington, New York/London, England: Kennikat Press, 1902, 1970

Wyse-Jackson, Peter. *Irish Trees and Shrubs.* Belfast, Northern Ireland: The Appletree Press Ltd, 1994

Donations would be gratefully accepted by:

The Tree Council of Ireland
(Comhairle Crann na hÉireann)
Royal Hospital
Dublin 8, Ireland

(telephone number +353 (0)1 679-0699)

INDEX

HOW TO ORDER

Name

Address

City, etc.

Country _____ Phone (with code) _____

Quan	Product	Price Each	Total
	Individual Oils (15 ml)*	£5.95/$9	
	Individual Essences (15 ml)*	£5.95/$9	
	Complete Set of (40) Individual Oils (£40/$60 freight)	£229.95/$345	
	Complete Set of (40) Individual Essences (£40/$60 freight)	£229.95/$345	
	Both Complete Individual Sets (80) (£80/$120 freight)	£450/$675	
	Systemic Oils (30 ml)*	£9/$13.50	
	Systemic Essences (30 ml)*	£9/$13.50	
	Complete Set of (12) Systemic Oils (£12/$18 freight)	£107/$161	
	Complete Set of (12) Systemic Essences (£12/$18 freight)	£107/$161	
	Both Complete Systemic Sets (24) (£24/$36 freight)	£210/$315	
	Poster – Small	£1.50/$2.25	
	Poster – Large	£4.50/$6.75	
	The Crane Bag	£8.50/$12	
	Set of Consultation Cards	£10.75/16.25	
	Brochures	FREE	
	Subtotal		
	Freight (Each item £1/$1.50. Set cost as stated)		
	Total		

*Please state which Oils and/or Essences you want.

We accept Cashier's Cheques, Bank Drafts, Money Orders

MasterCard and Visa also accepted:

Name on Card:

Card Number: Expiration Date:

Please mail to:

Celtic Tree Oils, Ltd., Carlingford, Co. Louth, Ireland
Phone: +353 (0)42-73793 or FAX: +353 (0)42-73839

Dealer and distributors inquiries are welcome!

Description/Individual	Oil	Essence
Ailim/Silver Fir		
Airne/Sloe		
Beit/Birch		
Cantabillae		
Cnó Capaill/Horse Chestnut		
Coad/Grove		
Coll/Hazel		
Conróis/Wild Rose		
Craobliat Corcra/Lilac		
Duir/Oak		
Eada/White Poplar		
Faibla Rua/Copper Beech		
Fearn/Alder		
Giúis/Pine		
Gort/Ivy		
Ioho/Yew		
Leamán/Elm		
Luis/Rowan		
Magdalen		
Meeshla		
Mór/The Sea		
Muin/Vine		
Ngetal/Reed		
Nuin/Ash		
Ohn/Furze		
Oir/Spindle		
Pagos/Beech		
Pís Cumra/Sweet Pea		
Quert/Apple		
Readóig/Bog Myrtle		
Ruis/Elder		
Saille Silte/Weeping Willow		
Saille/Willow		
Seiceamar/Sycamore		
Spiritual Rescue		
Straif/Blackthorn		
Tinne/Holly		
Uate/Hawthorn		
Uilleand/Honeysuckle		
Ur/Heather		
Total Quantities*		

*Please transfer Totals to first page of Order Form

Description/System	Oil	Essence
Circulatory		
Digestive		
Glandular		
Lymphatic		
Muscular		
Nervous		
Pancreatic		
Reproductive		
Respiratory & The Skin		
Sinusitis		
Skeletal		
Urinary		
Total Quantities*		

*Please transfer Totals to first page of Order Form

**Note: If ordering oils or essences, please include
all three pages of this form with your order.**

Thank you for your order.